Common Sense in Education

BOOKS BY HARRY KEMELMAN

Friday the Rabbi Slept Late
Saturday the Rabbi Went Hungry
Sunday the Rabbi Stayed Home
Nine Mile Walk
Common Sense in Education

Common Sense in Education

HARRY KEMELMAN

Crown Publishers, Inc., New York

LIBRARY OF CONGRESS CATALOG CARD NUMBER: 77–122762
PRINTED IN THE UNITED STATES OF AMERICA

Inquiries should be addressed to Crown Publishers, Inc., 419 Park Avenue South, New York, N.Y. 10016.

Published simultaneously in Canada by General Publishing Company Limited

Designed by Margery Kronengold

To the next generation—
so far represented by
Nina and **Jennifer**

Contents

By Way of Preface

My father was less than pleased when he learned of my intention to become a teacher. Then as now, it was a poorly paid profession. But this was not his chief reason for disliking it. In part, it was because a teacher had to work for an institution, a school or a college, and this meant being obligated to a president or a dean or a principal for his livelihood. He would have much preferred that I go into business—and of course he meant in business for myself—because a businessman was his own master. The major professions—law and medicine—were also acceptable, though they were somewhat lacking in other respects. Doctors, for whom he had great respect, were at the command of their patients and might even be called out in the middle of the night. For him this was a terrible intrusion on one's private time. As for the law, he thought of it as making capital out of the misfortunes of others. On the few occasions when he was himself involved either as a plaintiff or as a defendant in an action, he resented the lawyer's fee on the grounds that he was paying either to keep or to recover what was rightfully his; no matter how the case went, the lawyer's fee represented a net loss to him.

His chief objection to teaching, however, was that it ran counter to the talmudic principle that one should not use the Torah as a spade to dig with. Of course he was thinking of Torah in its widest possible sense, not as the Pentateuch or the Bible, but as learning in general. To use one's knowledge as a means of earning a living was to prostitute it, and a teacher, of course, was selling his knowledge.

"Then how about the doctor?" I objected. "He's making his living by selling his knowledge."

"The doctor is not selling his knowledge," he explained, "but rather the skill he derives from his knowledge. Besides, the doctor did not study medicine for himself; he studied it for you and for me—for society. Did he study medicine because he thought he himself might get sick and he wanted to know what to do in that case? Of course not. Some part of his study couldn't possibly apply, like women's disorders, or having a baby, or children's diseases. People get sick. This one catches a cold, that one gets a bellyache, another—God forbid—gets pneumonia. No one knows when sickness will strike or what sickness. If we were all to study how to take care of ourselves when we get sick, none of us would have time to do anything else. So he studies for us, and for this we should pay him. I'm sure he would rather read a book instead of his medical journals."

On the basis of the doctors I knew, I wasn't so sure.

"All right, but certainly he would rather deal with healthy, happy people than with the sick, miserable people he goes to see in the hospital. But he doesn't. He gives up his pleasures for our health, so for this we have to pay him."

"Then how does it differ for a teacher?"

"Come, let's be honest. When you read books—novels, plays,

poetry—did you do it in order to teach them to young people so they wouldn't have to read for themselves maybe? You studied these things for yourself because you liked them. And somebody else likes history. And another one likes mathematics or science. Teachers study these things for themselves, not for society. The learning that you do for yourself—that is Torah and it is not right to make your living from it."

"All right, how about a chemistry teacher? He studies chemistry and a doctor has to study chemistry; a biology teacher studies biology and the doctor has to study biology. Now are you saying that the doctor can make money from his study of chemistry and biology, but the science teacher must not?"

"Ah ha! The doctor you say *has to*. That's the difference. The chemistry teacher doesn't have to. The chemistry teacher studies chemistry because he likes it. Maybe the doctor likes it and maybe he doesn't. But in any case, he has to study it. Maybe they both take the same course, but for the doctor it is a necessity and for the teacher it is a pleasure."

I tried a different tack. "How about the golf pro, then? He certainly studied the game for pleasure, but it's his skill we're paying him for. You said it was all right in the case of the doctor."

He did not understand.

I explained the function of the golf pro, but he still did not understand. "Golf is a game, isn't it? It's a form of play, a pleasure? So does one take lessons to learn to play?"

"But if you want to learn to do it well . . ."

"So it means it's no pleasure unless you do it well? So that means you don't get pleasure from playing—only from winning."

"Then how about the music teacher? Doesn't he teach you something that you do for pleasure?" As a youngster I had been forced to study the violin.

"Ah, but that's different. If somebody didn't teach you how, you couldn't do it at all."

"How about chess? Don't tell me you don't enjoy winning."

"Of course I like to win. But I like just to play. And it is more pleasure to play with a good player and lose than to play with a poor player and win all the time."

"But suppose someone could teach you to play so that you could win all or even most of the time, even from the best players?"

He smiled and shook his head. "To play that well, you'd have to practice most of the day and every day. Is this something a man should do with his life?"

It crossed my mind that Aristotle had said that a gentleman should know how to play the flute, but not too well, but I resumed my attack. "All right, how about a rabbi? What he learned is certainly Torah and unquestionably he learned it for his own pleasure primarily, and yet he makes his living by it."

My father looked at me reproachfully, as though I had hit below the belt. As a matter of fact, most rabbis become uncomfortable when the question is raised. Normally they take refuge in the pilpul that they are not being paid for the religious work they do, but rather for the time it preempts, which could otherwise be spent in making a living. But my father offered the explanation that the real work of the rabbi was to hear cases presented to him and pass judgment on the basis of his knowledge of the Talmud. This was his traditional function. Here in America, however, he was expected to engage in a whole host of duties that were really not rabbinical. He was a kind of executive secretary to the temple organization, and since they took up his full time, he had to be paid; rarely, if ever, was he called upon to use his Talmudic knowledge.

"Then if he doesn't use it, what good is it? Are you saying that Torah is knowledge that has no practical value?"

"What good is it? It gives meaning to one's life as a man. It is what distinguishes the man from the beast. An animal learns, too, but an animal learns only practical things, useful knowledge. He learns where to go for food, what is dangerous and painful and how to avoid it—necessary, practical things. It is only man whose mind craves food for its own delight. And in this way, the mind and the soul develop and grow."

I mentioned a remark attributed to Albert Einstein that I had come across in my reading, something to the effect that pure research should be done on one's own time.

My father nodded. "Of course," he said, "if it were not on one's own time, it would not be pure."

It occurred to me at the time that my father's figure of speech, of the mind craving food for its sustenance so that it might grow and expand, was a good description of the educational process. In recent years, we have lost sight of the purpose of education as the development and improvement of the individual for his own benefit, and this has had a disastrous effect on our society. It is the situation in which we now find ourselves that I propose to examine in the chapters that follow.

CHAPTER 1

The Problem

The student strikes and campus rebellions that have become common in recent years present a curious sociological phenomenon. Strikes of one sort or another are endemic to our society. In addition to those of organized labor, countless protests by a variety of groups also develop into strikes. There are consumer strikes against high prices, taxpayers' rebellions against excessive taxation, boycotts of the merchandise of a particular country, sit-ins by the residents of a neighborhood against the seizure of their homes by eminent domain, and, as happened recently in my area, a baby-carriage blockade of a road to prevent its being used by a procession of lumbering trucks carrying fill to extend the local airport.

Almost invariably these strikes make sense to the disinterested onlooker. He may consider the demands of the strikers unwise or futile, unreasonable or unfair, shortsighted or even harmful to the striker himself in the long run, but he can understand the reason for the strike. The man who holds the bulldozers at bay with a shotgun to prevent the demolition of his house may be a nut, but we can understand the reason for his action. Similarly, we may regard as unwise to the point of being suicidal a strike that forces the company out of business, but we can understand the strikers' wanting a bigger share of the pie. Even the strikes to maintain and extend featherbedding practices that we the consumers will have to pay for are understandable. We may be outraged by strikes by policemen and firemen and garbage collectors and bus operators—but we can understand them. In all cases, the strikers want something that is to their advantage, albeit frequently to the disadvantage of the rest of us.

What is curious about the campus strikes, however, is that frequently the strikers gain no benefit or advantage even if they win; the protests are presumably for the benefit of someone else. But even when they do stand to gain, or when the strike is against a specific grievance, the violence is out of all proportion to the benefit to be derived or the grievance suffered.

At one school, the students mounted a protest because the administration had accepted a half-million-dollar endowment for a school of nursing from someone reputed to be a slumlord, and—shades of Bernard Shaw and *Major Barbara!*—forced the university to return the money. At one school, white students struck because there was segregation of Negro students in the college dormitories; at another because there wasn't.

There were strikes, picketing, militant action of one sort or another at a number of colleges to prevent recruitment of seniors for officers' training programs in the armed services, as well as action against the recruiting on campus by agents of a chemical firm with a government contract for the manufacture of napalm.

There was student action against one university because its stock portfolio contained investments in South African corporations; there were protests without number over the firing of various teachers; there were protests over individual courses in the curriculum and over the absence of certain courses, like Swahili or programs of black studies. At one point in the student war at Berkeley a battle was waged over the right of students to carry obscene signs and parade them about the campus. And the Columbia protest had its inception over the question of whether the college had been sufficiently generous to the residents of the neighboring black community in the matter of a contemplated gymnasium to which the neighbors would have access.

There were numerous actions over censorship of student publications, frequently on the question of the right of the authorities to prevent publication of libelous scurrilities or obscenities. There were attacks against the authorities' presuming to exercise any supervision over the sexual mores of the student body. And of course, when student action ended in punishment of the leaders, there were secondary strikes calling for amnesty. More recently the strikes have been for the purpose of establishing the rights of the students to a voice in what has been regarded as purely administrative matters: the hiring and firing of teachers, the form of the curriculum, the admissions policy.

Long lists of demands are presented and labeled nonnegotiable; there is a time limit for compliance. There is no consideration whether the president or the dean has the authority to agree to them or the power to effect the required changes, or even whether the mere mechanics can be worked out in the time allotted. The word is, Do it! Do it instanter! Or else!

I do not suggest that none of these is a just grievance. It is also possible that the newspapers and the radio and the TV from which I and the reader, no doubt, get our knowledge of the events may not be presenting the student argument properly. They may be slanting their coverage in favor of the administration and against the students. And one can always argue that although the actual problem appears minor there is always a sacred principle at stake, like freedom of the press or academic freedom or social justice. But in general, and making all possible allowances, the extent and violence of the reaction still seem entirely out of keeping with the significance of the ostensible cause.

In the face of the numerous exposés of the questionable practices of some of our most prestigious corporations, is it proper to force the college to refuse a donation of half a million dollars at the expense of new and improved facilities for the school of nursing—and it might be interesting to know what the prospective students of the school thought—because the donor is thought to have made his money not illegally but in a way that the students disapprove of?

Since it is common knowledge that there is scarcely a large industrial corporation that is not engaged in the manufacture of matériel for the war, is it reasonable to mount a campaign to prevent the recruitment of seniors by one chemical company that has devoted a tiny portion of its production to the manufacture of napalm, which, unlike tanks and shells, has industrial as well as military uses?

If the Officers Training Program involved shanghaiing unwilling recruits, violent student reaction would be understandable. But since the program is purely voluntary, and no one need sign up who doesn't want to, the assumption is that the activists are protecting their fellow students against their own weakness. The same is true of the attack on the ROTC program. Curiously, opposition does not appear on those campuses where the great majority of the student body is enrolled, but rather in those schools where only a tiny minority participates in the program.

"But all this proves they're idealistic, doesn't it?" a thoughtful father might ask. "I mean, they're not doing any of this for themselves. They *are* the brightest generation so far, aren't they? I mean, you hear that from all kinds of experts—that they're idealistic and smart and knowledgeable. Of course, you wonder about this business of wrecking offices, and then there's that college president who got a heart attack. . . . But they're young and I guess sometimes a little thoughtless. And when you're involved in a row, sometimes things happen. But they're not selfish. I mean, they're doing this for—well, for others. . . . I mean, they're essentially idealistic. Look what they did in the McCarthy campaign. That shows there's good stuff in them, doesn't it? Well, doesn't it?"

The tone is anxious. He wants so much to believe that it is all for the good, that it is a manifestation of a fine, high spirit of idealism and honesty and sincerity, because otherwise his investment in getting his son into a good college has obviously failed.

Another peculiar aspect of the student rebellion is the kind of student who takes part. No doubt, studies are being prepared, if they have not already been, complete with statistical tables so dear to the hearts of social scientists, showing the characteristics of the typical student activist. But merely a casual reading of the press reports suggests that most of them come from middle-class backgrounds. This makes their rebellion even more difficult to understand, since this is the class that is distinguished by its foresight and prudence and caution. These are neither young aristocrats who might quixotically hazard all on a gesture, nor are they of the poor. No, these are the sons of doctors and lawyers and accountants and corporation executives and teachers and businessmen.

They know that the comparatively pleasant surroundings that they grew up in are not something that they will inherit. The son of the millionaire may not need a degree to get a good job and he may not need a job to continue the standard of living that he is accustomed to. But the youth of middle-class background can expect no inheritance that will keep him going indefinitely. He will have to earn his living by his own efforts.

The sanctions that may be applied by the college authorities to recalcitrant students are serious. Admission to a college these days is hard enough; expulsion can be little short of disastrous. White collar jobs these days demand a college degree, so the young man who has no degree is under a severe handicap. And the young man who has been dismissed from a college for disciplinary reasons will not readily find the doors of other colleges open to him.

Right now there is an additional penalty. College students are of draft age but have a deferment from military service because of their student status. Once the student is dismissed from the college, however, even if he is merely suspended for a year, his student status is subject to review and he may be called to active service. Nevertheless, in spite of these serious dangers, both immediate and for the long run, we find that students have been willing to take these risks.

It is this that baffles our understanding and makes it impossible for us to laugh off the current riots as the contemporary equivalent of the panty raids and goldfish swallowing of an earlier period, as a manifestation of the high spirits and instability of youth.

This homely example suggests a possible explanation. Recently, my daughter and her husband, having occasion to go away for a few days, left their two children with us. Most of the work fell to my wife, of course, but I could not escape my share of the burden of keeping the elder, aged three, amused. Although Nina's vocabulary is somewhat limited and she is not too sure about verb tenses, she is quite articulate and even fluent for her age and we were able to hold long "grown-up" conversations that she seemed to enjoy. We had what social workers call "a good relationship."

Hence, when she burst into tears for no apparent reason, I was understandably nonplussed. She had awakened from her afternoon nap, and I was trying to put on her shoes when the floodgates opened. In vain I pointed out that since she had learned to talk, there was no longer any need for her to cry: she could *tell* me what troubled her. I pleaded with her. Quite possibly I threatened her—with the loss of some privilege or other. I suggested a number of possibilities: Did her tummy hurt? Was her foot asleep? Would she prefer her sneakers? Finally, pointing to a spot some three inches above the reach of the shoe, in a tear-choked voice she informed me that she had hurt her leg. The incident had occurred some time ago, and the scratch had been barely noticeable. Now, weeks later, I could not see the slightest mark or scar. Nevertheless, with my reading glasses, I gravely examined the area, and affixed a Band-aid to the place indicated.

Of course I realized it was no recurrent pain from a scratch sustained weeks earlier that was troubling her. She could not tell me what was really troubling her because it was far beyond her understanding and the capacity of her vocabulary: that she found the bed she had been sleeping in and the surroundings strange; that, on awakening, the sight of me rather than her mother was momentarily inexplicable; that she was indignant at having been abandoned by her parents and was uncertain of what would happen next and of the future in general.

Having assuaged her weltschmerz in a flood of tears, she was now prepared to rejoin the world of her grandparents and needed only some reason for her tears that was acceptable to the crass adult mind. This the weeks-old injury afforded.

This phenomenon is not confined to little girls just learning to talk. On the contrary, it is an all-too-human characteristic. When the vexations of life—an unaccustomed malaise, a momentary annoyance with one's wife or a neighbor, the onset of a sudden fear having little foundation in fact—are too subtle or in combination become too complicated to articulate, or perhaps appear too minor to justify voiced complaint even to oneself, then it is not uncommon to lash out at something that one *can* conceive and understand and articulate.

To the onlooker, the student reaction appears incomprehensible or untimely or exaggerated just as, to me, did little Nina's tears over her old bruise. But that does not mean that the outcry is without justification; only that we must look elsewhere for the cause. Otherwise we would have to assume that a whole generation has suddenly become paranoid.

Let us delineate our problem carefully. The rioting, although sooner or later involving the entire university, is largely a function of the undergraduate college of liberal arts. There is always a small core of professed revolutionaries, the leaders, who start things. We are not concerned with them. In all groups there are extremists. But by the very nature of group organization, the extremists, the fringe, are always a small portion of the whole and are usually disregarded by the rest. Their presence on the campus today is nothing new.

What is new in the present situation is that, in school after school, the moderate center of the student body has listened to them avidly when they would normally have jeered and scoffed; has rushed to their defense when they have been attacked; has followed their lead in actions that would normally have been repugnant to them.

So now, to restate our problem: Why is it that students of middle-class backgrounds, largely those concentrating in the humanities in our liberal arts colleges, so readily follow revolutionary leaders in courses that are not only normally repugnant to them, but that are contrary to their best interests both immediate and for the future?

CHAPTER 2

The Liberal Arts College—Then and Now

In 1926 when I matriculated at Boston University, tuition was three hundred dollars a year. Give or take fifty dollars, it was the tuition rate of most of the privately endowed colleges in the Northeast. My textbooks could not have cost more than twenty dollars per year. In science courses there was a laboratory fee of ten dollars to cover breakage, a portion of which was returned at the end of the year; the amount retained by the college always seemed to be far in excess of the cost of the breakage one had actually incurred. There were one or two minor fees, perhaps a dollar for a locker at the gymnasium, perhaps another dollar for a Student Activities fee. In addition I needed money for lunches and carfare. I was under no expense for board and lodging since I lived at home.

I had gone to the Boston Latin School, and from there most

of the boys went on to matriculate at Harvard. Their expenses were comparable to mine, since they too lived at home. For people in my social and economic class—my father was a small businessman in comfortable circumstances—that was the rule: you went to a local college if there was one available, and you lived at home. Living in Boston, I was fortunate in having a choice of several schools. In any case, all colleges located in or near a city drew a large portion of their students from the surrounding community.

Salaries and incomes were of course much lower in those days, but for those who were living at home and whose parents were in comfortable circumstances, college was not a great drain on the family finances. Those who had to live at school were subject to additional fees for board and lodging that might amount to six or seven hundred dollars a year, and this added to the tuition fee *could* very well constitute a heavy burden on their parents.

Admission to college was by way of examinations given by the colleges themselves or by the College Entrance Examination Board. The usual requirements were passing marks in fifteen units of approved subjects where major subjects counted for three units and minor subjects for two. Most students took the College Board exams given in the spring. They were largely three-hour examinations in each subject and covered intensively the material studied. In foreign language examinations, for example, there were questions on vocabulary and grammar, long passages to translate into English, and long English passages to put into the foreign language. In the English exam, there were searching questions on the reading one had done, and these were to be answered in essay form. In addition, there was testing on vocabulary, spelling, grammar, and, most important, one or more compositions had to be written on subjects given. Some colleges required in addition to the three-hour written science examination a laboratory demonstration as well, and the student not only set up the apparatus and performed his experiment, but was quizzed orally by a proctor on the principles involved.

Some colleges also accepted applicants without examination on the basis of certification by the headmasters of their schools that they were in the top fifth of their class or had grades that averaged B or better.

No one who passed his College Board exams was worried about being admitted to college. Only those who had failed in one or more of their exams were nervous about their chances, and they hoped to be admitted on probation. Some schools, because of limited facilities, had begun to limit their enrollment. In New England, rumor had it that Dartmouth had embarked on a policy of limiting their enrollment to a certain type—the well-rounded all-American boy—and required each applicant for admission to be interviewed and recommended by one of their alumni. There were also rumors that some colleges had set a percentage limit on Jewish students.

To be turned down by a college was no great tragedy; one had only to apply to another. Like the rest of my class at the Latin School, I had applied for admission to Harvard. When I was turned down, I was surprised but not particularly upset. Shortly before registration day, I applied to Boston University. The registrar, remarking that it was late in the season, asked me if I had previously applied elsewhere, and I replied that I had and had been turned down by Harvard. Inasmuch as I had passed seventeen units of College Board exams, the registrar was curious as to why I had been refused and suggested that it might be worth my while to find out.

I did not care too much one way or the other. Admission to college was not then the life-or-death matter it is today. In fact, I had a rather hoity-toity, cavalier attitude toward college study. The general feeling of the time was that college was primarily a place where immature boys wore funny hats and were engaged largely in having a good time. The great writers and intellectuals of the period, most of whom were in the stable of Mencken's *American Mercury,* of which I was a devoted reader, were almost all self-taught and I was all too inclined to follow in their footsteps. But it seemed worth a ten-cent carfare, if only for the opportunity it might give me to put the august Harvard establishment on the defensive. So I journeyed to Cambridge and at the Admissions Office asked to see the chairman of the committee.

I had some idea why I had been refused. My high school career had been hectic. I had left the Latin School for disciplinary reasons, had gone to another high school in the city, and then had returned to the Latin School. In the meantime, I had taken a number of College Board exams that I had no right to take since I had never taken the courses they were presumed to test. I had studied the material at home. For example, I had taken the College Board in second year German although I had never taken a course in German. Instead I studied German grammar by myself and relied on my knowledge of Yiddish for sufficient vocabulary to see me through the translation passages.

Needless to say, I got no satisfaction from the chairman of the admissions committee, but I spent a pleasant hour there and was not sorry I had come. After I had been at Boston University for a few months, I decided that I was glad matters had turned out as they had, and four years later when I entered Harvard Graduate School for advanced work in my field, this feeling was confirmed. The college of liberal arts at Boston University, unlike Harvard, was a friendly place where the instructors were primarily interested in teaching and were not under pressure to publish or do research.

The point of all this is that my refusal at Harvard was not a traumatic experience either for me or for my folks. I would not even have been overly concerned if I had not been admitted to Boston University either. If one wanted to study, there were any number of other possibilities. One could go directly to a law school, for example. Or one could get a job and take courses at night. It was no great tragedy not to go to college at all. One could study by oneself. Jobs, though not plentiful, were available, and not having a college degree was no bar to employment. Or one could, perhaps, with small capital start a small business of one's own. Most businesses at the time were small.

There was no pressure to go to college. No one *had* to go. Even those who were interested in one of the professions as a career did not have to go to a liberal arts college first. There were any number of law schools that accepted students directly from high school, and in Massachusetts the statutes still permitted reading in a lawyer's office in place of attending a law school as preparation for the bar exam, although I never knew anyone who had done so. Even acceptable medical schools and schools of dentistry did not require four years of liberal arts training. It was possible to gain admission to any number of medical schools by taking a year or two of premedical study. As for accounting, only later was it regarded as a proper field for inclusion in the university family; if you wanted to be a certified public accountant, the normal preparation was by way of one of the many private business schools where anyone having a high school diploma or its equivalent—and equivalency received broad interpretation—was admitted. As for business administration, advertising, journalism, hotel management, theatrical arts, designing—these were not regarded as the province of the university or the college, except perhaps in the large state colleges of the Midwest, and this was one of the many characteristics of these institutions that fortified educators in my section of the country in the belief that the state must never be permitted a toehold in the control and direction of higher education.

Most colleges, in fact all except the few with huge endowments, were actively engaged in recruiting students. Representatives of the colleges would travel to the high schools to make their pitch to the seniors. College presidents were engaged in selling the idea of the liberal arts college. The argument was that the lifetime earnings of college graduates were higher than the lifetime earnings of those without a college education, in spite of the handicap of starting their earning careers four years later.

If one did not need a college degree to get a decent job, and one did not absolutely need it to go to one of the professional schools, why did students go at all? Who did go?

Some went because their main interest was the professional

school, and they wanted to go to the more highly reputed which *did* require an academic degree for admission. They tended to take as many courses as they could in fields closely allied to the professions they were planning to enter. For them, the liberal arts college was largely a temporary impediment, a hurdle they had to overcome to be admitted to the professional school of their choice. If the fine professional school had not required liberal arts study, they would not have bothered with it.

Then there were the football players, for by the twenties, college football had become one of the principal products of the institution. There were no professional teams in those days except perhaps those which played on local playgrounds and made their expenses by passing the hat around. College football was the big thing, and tickets to the games of ancient "traditional rivals" like Harvard and Yale were sold by scalpers for as much as fifty dollars apiece. Many a Harvard student of my acquaintance paid an installment on his tuition by the sale of his allotted two tickets. The student who came to play football was a much more common phenomenon in the giant state colleges of the South and the West and the Midwest than in the much smaller colleges of New England. Recruited by the coach, their expenses paid by football scholarships, entrance examinations waived or winked at, their study and classwork and course examinations regarded by the entire college family as mere formalities, these brawny young men were purely and simply employees of the college. If their actual pay, the scholarship money, was small for the work done and the risks taken, it was compensated for by the academic degree granted after four years and the opportunities afforded for publicity which could later on be converted to lucrative selling jobs. Any academic knowledge acquired was purely accidental.

Then there were the sons of rich men who after graduating from prep school were still not ready to settle down to a soft job in their fathers' business. They went because college offered them an opportunity to spend a few more years not too arduously before they assumed their share of the burden of the world's work. It was also felt that college afforded them an opportunity to make contacts that might later be useful.

This last was also the rationalization of those from the middle class who were not primarily interested in study. From the point of view of their parents, the college, the liberal arts college that is, conferred social status and economic prestige. A boy at law school or medical school or an engineering school was merely a boy learning a profession by which he would later make his living. In that sense he was similar to a boy going to a trade school. True, the training was longer and far more costly, but the assumption was that the eventual monetary return would justify the present expenditure of time and money. An investment in money would return money.

By contrast, the student at the college of liberal arts was not learning anything that guaranteed a financial return. But to relieve a son from his share of the family burden, to maintain him in idleness for four years, and this at considerable expense, was proof of the financial success and stability of the parent.

"And what is your boy doing now, Mr. Smith?"

"Oh, he's at college."

"He's going to be a lawyer? Or a doctor?"

"No, I don't think so. When he gets through he'll be coming into my business."

"So what is he studying at college?"

"Oh, just a general education."

"Four years to spend for nothing? It must be pretty expensive."

"Well, it's not cheap, I can tell you."

Thorsten Veblen's theories of conspicuous waste establishing social prestige were all very well, but in middle-class America the waste must not be too frivolous, so Mr. Smith would add, "I figure the friendships and contacts he'll make while he's there will come in handy later on." And his interrogator would go away with the idea that not only was Smith doing well enough in his business to keep his son at college for four years but that he was a pretty smart man who had an eye to the future. For whom would young Smith meet at college but others like himself, the sons of rich fathers? Who else could afford it? And later on when young Smith would take over, what was more useful than to know bankers, manufacturers, wholesalers, by their first names? There were no doubt other reasons as well: "Because you're a Jones and the Jones men always go to Siwash, that's why." Or even, "Because Dad was getting married again, and he thought it might be a little awkward me being there at home, and I agreed with him, so we thought the best thing would be for me to go off to college until things kind of settle down."

But all these were the exceptional cases. Most students at the liberal arts college went because they wanted to study and learn.

To be sure, motives are never unmixed and intentions are frequently changed or forgotten. The student who sought sanctuary in the college from his father's business—or from his father—might become interested in Latin poetry or English history and then go on to the graduate school for his doctorate and eventually end up teaching, or he might decide to study for one of the professions. And conversely, the student who went to college because he wanted to learn might get bogged down in the fascinating hurly-burly of fraternity activity or campus politics or intercollegiate athletics and at the end of the four years have nothing to show for it except perhaps some contacts to whom he would later try to sell stocks and bonds, or insurance.

As far as the general public was concerned, the liberal arts college was a fun place. How could it be otherwise when the major question that agitated the incoming freshman was whether to join a fraternity or not? When his concern about adjustment to college life centered around freshman hazing? When the names of the football players were better known than those of the most distinguished professors, or of the college president?

The movies, as the popular art of the time, give a clue to the general feeling about college. For a while, there was a whole cycle of college movies. Yet I cannot remember a single college movie, and I think I saw most of them—for a while there seemed to be no other kind—where the plot did not revolve around the football team or where the inside of a classroom was shown. If there was a professor in the picture, he was usually a comic figure.

The movies tend to oversimplify. The overwhelming majority of the students did not come to play football, nor even to cheer the team and bask in the reflected glory of its successes. They came because they felt that what they had got in high school and preparatory school was not enough and they wanted more. For most of them, the liberal arts college was not a doorway to the graduate and professional schools; the A.B. was for them a terminal degree. After graduation, they planned on getting jobs, or working in the family business, or starting one of their own. They viewed their academic education as a means of broadening their minds to give them greater understanding.

Not all profited, of course, as suggested earlier. Many did little studying, and then went on to their life's work with little to show for their four years except a sentimental loyalty to their college and a collection of nostalgic memories that were trotted out at college reunions on the order of the time they locked Professor Jones in the chapel bell tower.

But the movies were right in one thing, however: college life was pleasant and frequently fun. For the many who lived at home, it involved no great expense. Consequently there was no feeling on the part of the average student that his going to college involved the family in ruinous expenditure entailing unpleasant economies on the part of his parents. And therefore there was no sense of guilt on his part if he did not repay their efforts by making the Dean's List. Pressure was minimal. It was no great problem to get in and there was no thought that one's life was ruined if one failed to stay in. There were plently of other alternatives. The college student was there on a voluntary basis. He came, for whatever reason—but he came because he wanted to come. No one forced him to go; neither his parents nor the subconscious pressure of his circle, nor the thought that it was necessary for making a living.

How different is the scene today! College has become an absolute necessity for young people of the middle class, and from those of the blue collar class as well who want to rise above the social and economic status of their parents. In the large corporations, and they constitute an ever-increasing portion of our economy, a college degree is an absolute requirement for all jobs that lead to advancement. Like the army, where the enlisted man can rise no higher than sergeant major, the large corporation rarely advances workers from the ranks to executive or administrative positions. The master sergeant who has been in the army for twenty years will take his orders from a shavetail still not certain which hand to salute with, even when he has to tell the lieutenant what orders to give. Jobs that call for no specialized training but that are executive or administrative in nature, or from which the executive and administrative ranks are filled, are limited to men with college degrees. So the young man who has a normal desire to occupy a position of responsibility someday must of necessity go to college even though he has no interest in higher learning. It has become a kind of initiation rite.

Nor are there the alternatives that existed forty years ago. Young men cannot go to a professional school directly from high school; job opportunities are ever more and more limited; and starting a small business in the face of the competition of big business is ever more and more hazardous.

Perhaps the most aggravating aspect of the situation is, however, that the more necessary college training became, the more difficult it became to gain admission. Getting into college these days is a traumatic experience for both the applicant and his parents. One cannot start the effort too early: it is important to go to a good grade school in order to get the proper preparation to do well in high school. But even high grades in high school are of little value unless the applicant also gets high grades on the College Board examinations. And even here, the student has no idea of where he stands with the college he is interested in, because there is no longer a passing grade in the College Boards which he must clear, but merely a position on a curve; and his chosen college might consider it insufficient for their standards for that year. Even if he gets the highest possible marks, the college may still reject him on the grounds that he does not display in his extracurricular activities the qualities they think they want. So he applies to a number of schools in the hope that at least one will admit him. And when he is finally admitted, he and his parents are so relieved that for the moment they hardly think of the expense—which can be enormous and crippling. Tuition alone at some of the private foundations runs to $2,500 a year and more. Board, lodging, books, travel to and from home during the vacations will add up to a like amount. Five thousand dollars a year, and none of it tax deductible! Who can afford it?

The crowning blow is that after all this effort and worry and expense, college is no longer a particularly pleasant place to be. Whether it is a feeling of guilt at the thought of the sacrifices his parents are making to meet his college bills, or the amount of work that is required of him to maintain passing marks and the lack of free time that results, or the tensions induced by the necessity of making a sufficiently good record to get into a graduate school—for more and more students think of college as merely another hurdle to be overcome on the road to the professional school where they will finally learn something that will enable them to earn a living—the fact is that the college student of today does not seem to be happy.

I see it in his face and in his carriage and in his behavior. I see it in what he does for relaxation. But it is also obvious in the statistics of nervous breakdowns, suicides, and most of all in the number who transfer from year to year, hoping no doubt that at another college things will be different. In some colleges, the number of transfers is more than half as great as the number who enter as freshmen.

CHAPTER 3

What It Is

The question naturally arises as to what good a liberal education is. Granted that study sharpens the mind or improves it somehow or other, why can't it be improved through the study of something useful? Why can't the student improve his mind and learn a profession at the same time? Presumably, the young man who went to an engineering school had his mind improved by the training and discipline, but he also had a job on graduation.

The question is echoed today in a slightly different form now that the A.B. degree *does* act as a ticket of admittance to a host of jobs. Today the cry is for "relevancy." The attitude of the student is frequently that the liberal arts courses lack relevance. Instead of Latin, why not study a living language that might come in handy some day, like Russian or Chinese? Why study European history when the time could be spent studying the problems of the city? Why study mathematics, which one will never use, when one could study accounting—which is certain to come in handy? For that matter, why not cooking instead of chemistry, auto mechanics instead of physics?

I think the great majority of college students of my day had an instinctive knowledge that the liberal arts college was in some way different from the more utilitarian schools of higher learning. They viewed the professional school as narrowing the focus of the mind; the liberal arts college broadened it.

In law school, all courses were related to law just as in medical school all courses had some relation to the practice of medicine. To be sure, they afforded the mind training and exercise, as does all study, but the liberal arts curriculum embraced the entire field of knowledge and hence served not only to exercise and train the mind, but to expand it as well.

Faculties not only made a distinction between education and training but, like my father, had an instinctive belief that there was some special virtue in study that had no predictable or discernible utility: dead languages like Latin and Greek were somehow better for the mind than French or German; algebra and geometry, which they would probably never use, were somehow better than bookkeeping and accounting; chemistry and physics and astronomy were of greater significance in their total development than auto mechanics and electrical wiring.

To understand the nature of the liberal arts college and its function in our society, it is important to understand the difference between *education* and *training*.

Training is intended primarily for the service of society; education is primarily for the individual. Society needs doctors, lawyers, engineers, teachers to perform specific tasks necessary to its operation, just as it needs carpenters and plumbers and stenographers. Training supplies the immediate and specific needs of society so that the work of the world may continue. And these needs, our training centers—the professional and trade schools—fill. But although education is for the improvement of the individual, it also serves society by providing a leavening of men of understanding, of perception, and wisdom. They are our intellectual leaders, the critics of our culture, the defenders of our free traditions, the instigators of our progress. They serve society by examining its function, appraising its needs, and criticizing its direction. They may be earning their livings by practicing one of the professions, or in pursuing a trade, or by engaging in business enterprise. They may be rich or poor. They may occupy positions of power and prestige, or they may be engaged in some humble employment. Without them, however, society either disintegrates or else becomes an anthill.

The difference between the two types of study is like the difference between the discipline and exercise in a professional baseball training camp and that of a Y gym. In the one, the recruit is training to become a professional baseball player who will make a living and serve society by playing baseball; in the other, he is training only to improve his own body and musculature. The training at the baseball camp is all relevant. The recruit may spend hours practicing how to slide into second base, not because it is a particularly useful form of calisthenics but because it is relevant to the game. The exercise would stop if the rules were changed so that sliding to a base was made illegal. Similarly, the candidate for the pitching staff spends a lot of time throwing a baseball, not because it will improve his physique —it may have quite the opposite effect—but because pitching is to be his principal function on the team. At the Y gym, exercises have no such relevance. The intention is to strengthen the body in general, and when the members sit down on the floor with their legs outstretched and practice touching their fingers to their toes, it is not because they hope to become galley slaves, perhaps the only occupation where that particular exercise would be relevant.

In general, relevancy is a facet of training rather than of education. What is taught at law school is the present law of the land, not the Napoleonic Code or even the archaic laws that have been scratched from the statute books. And at medical school, too, it is modern medical practice that is taught, that which is relevant to conditions today. And the plumber and the carpenter and the electrician and the mason learn only what is relevant to the practice of their respective trades in this day with the tools and materials that are presently available and that conform to the building code.

In the liberal arts college, on the other hand, the student is encouraged to explore new fields and old fields, to wander down the bypaths of knowledge. There the teaching is concerned with major principles, and its purpose is to change the student, to make him something different from what he was before, just as the purpose of the Y gym is to make a fat man into a thin one, or a strong one out of a weak one.

Clearly the two types of learning overlap. Just as the baseball recruit gets rid of excess weight and tightens his muscles at the baseball camp and thereby profits even if he does not make the team, so the law student sharpens his mind and broadens his understanding, even if he subsequently fails the bar exam and goes on to make his living in an entirely different kind of work. His study of law gives him an understanding of the rules under which our society functions and his practice in solving legal problems gives him an understanding of fine distinctions.

On the other hand, the Y member, whose original reason for joining may have been solely to get himself in shape, may get caught up in the institution's basketball program and find that his skill has developed to the point where he can play the game professionally. Similarly, the student who undertakes a course of study merely because it interests him and he wants to know more about it may find that it has commercial value. He has studied a foreign language and literature in order to understand the society that produced it, and then he may find that his special knowledge enables him to get a job as a translator. Or he may find that while his knowledge of chemistry is not of professional caliber, it is still sufficient to give him preference in a particular job over someone who lacks even that modicum of knowledge of the subject. But these are accidental and incidental. In general, certain courses of study are for the service of society and other courses are for self-improvement. In the hierarchy of our educational system, the former are the function of our professional schools and the latter are the function of the college of liberal arts.

There is no pretense that study in a liberal arts college will equip the student to hold a job that he otherwise could not hold. Even in the twenties when college presidents were trying to sell their schools on the grounds that liberal arts education would increase one's lifetime earnings, there was no suggestion that this course of study would qualify the student for a particular job. By that time, the system of concentration in a particular field had been well-nigh universally accepted, yet there was no thought that this concentration constituted professional expertise. The intention of the plan of concentration in a single field was merely to give focus to the course of study and was an attempt to overcome the major fault in the free elective course-credit system. So the system of major and minor concentration was introdued. But it is indicative of the nature of the college of liberal arts, and of the awareness that the curriculum must not become a professional course of study, that along with the introduction of the system of concentration, there was also instituted a system of diversification. That is, in order to qualify for the bachelor's degree, the student not only had to show major and minor concentration (usually a minimum of thirty hours, about a quarter of the total, for the major and fifteen hours for the minor), but lest he pursue courses in only these two fields, he had to show a certain number of hours in each of the other major fields of study.

We have come to think of the professional school as a graduate school and of the liberal arts college as an undergraduate school and hence a kind of preparatory school; this is essentially a recent development and is not based on the fact that one is more difficult than the other. Medical and law schools are largely graduate institutions; but business, engineering, and journalism schools and military academies are usually undergraduate schools, although in some universities the business school has become a graduate school requiring a bachelor's degree for admission. Education or teachers' training schools also seem to be in a fair way of being similarly upgraded in the not distant future.

In Massachusetts, it was not until the early thirties that preliminary liberal arts study was made a requirement for the study of law, and then only two years of such study were required. Inasmuch as the law was passed when the Depression was at its nadir, and inasmuch as the great majority of state legislators were lawyers, there is the likelihood that its passage was motivated not by the feeling that the study of law necessitated preliminary liberal arts study, but purely in an effort to limit the number of competitors in the profession. (So too, the history of the general political activity of the American Medical Association suggests that the same motive may have been behind the upgrading of medical schools to the graduate level.) If the legal profession improved markedly as a result of this upgrading, there is nothing in contemporary life to suggest it.

Originally, the liberal arts study of those who planned to go on to the medical school was essentially premedical in nature, with much concentration in the sciences, particularly chemistry and the biological sciences. At some medical schools, notably Harvard, it is suggested that the student concentrate in some field other than the scientific, and the thinking now is that the student who has majored in French literature and minored in music has a better chance of acceptance at medical school than the student who has majored in biology.

This suggests that while liberal arts study may be desirable for a doctor or a lawyer—indeed why would it not be desirable for a carpenter or plumber?—it is not a *necessary* preliminary to the study of law or medicine. Without a doubt, since the college graduate is four years older than the high school graduate, and hence likely to be more mature, he will probably do better at these professional studies. No doubt four years spent in any kind of study helps the student get practice in the art of study; but there is no reason to assume that a course in Freshman English or elementary sociology helps in the study of anatomy more than the other way around.

CHAPTER 4

How It Works

Obviously, to have its effect, the liberal arts program must be something other than a bunch of unrelated and useless courses. The question is: What is it and how does it work? How does it achieve its effect?

Originally, the seven liberal arts that constituted the program comprised the whole of formal knowledge, and the ideal of the educated man was one who had taken all knowledge as his province. But this was when the sum total of human knowledge was small enough to be encompassed in a course of study of a few years. As knowledge expanded, the theory developed that the liberal arts program achieved its effect by a kind of bird's-eye view of the entire field, or perhaps a sampling of the various phases of what was known.

I find this explanation unsatisfactory. In the present state of our knowledge, the sampling in each field would have to be so small as to be useless, and the bird's-eye view of so vast an area would mark only the very largest of the landmarks. But when we analyze the requirements of the liberal arts curriculum, how the course must be run, we are able to arrive at an explanation of how it achieves its effect. We see that the intention is not to give a sampling of the different areas of knowledge, but rather to give an understanding of the various *tests of truth*.

Most colleges arrange their courses for credit purposes into six or eight broad areas or groups, and the student is required to take two or three courses in each group in addition to the five or six that he will take in his field of concentration. The grouping scheme may differ slightly from college to college, but the basic plan is the same. One group consists of courses in the physical sciences—physics, chemistry, and astronomy; in some schools the biological sciences are included with them. Another group is the social sciences—psychology, economics, sociology, government, education, anthropology. Sometimes history is also included in this group and sometimes the history courses make up a separate group of their own. Then there is the group that includes philosophy and formal logic and mathematics. In some schools mathematics is grouped with the exact sciences and philosophy with psychology. Another group is the arts—music, painting, and literature. And finally there is a language group sometimes including all languages and sometimes divided so that Latin and Greek are a separate group combined with classical studies. Some colleges have English language and literature as a group separate from that of the other languages even where distinction is made between modern languages and classical languages. At least one course used to be required in all colleges—Freshman English—but there is a tendency now in more progressive institutions to permit the student to anticipate this course either by examination or by demonstrating better than average ability in his College Board English exam. Some few colleges require all students, regardless of their field of concentration, to take a survey course in English literature on the assumption that all students whatever their special interests should know something of their own literature.

The point is that there is no single test of truth for all phenomena; truth is multiform and depends on the material we are dealing with. The various courses in each group, however, make use of the same test of truth because the material dealt with is basically similar. So the study of physics while it gives no knowledge of chemistry, nevertheless involves the same test for truth: that is, 100 percent conformance. In physics as in chemistry or astronomy nothing less than that which is 100 percent predictable can be considered a scientific truth. Only that is accepted as truth that can be tested repeatedly and that will always present the identical answer. The exact sciences like physics and chemistry can establish 100 percent conformance as their criterion of truth because they deal with nonliving matter and hence with matter that is or can be made 100 percent homogeneous. All variables can be either eliminated or measured and accounted for and all conditions of an experiment can be duplicated exactly. The results, and methods, would be quite different in chemistry, for example, if there were no pure chemicals and the effect of the impurities could not be calculated.

In the biological sciences, on the other hand, 100 percent conformity is practically impossible since the science deals with living forms, no two of which are ever exactly the same. One hundred percent conformity is therefore impossible since the material involved is not homogeneous.

In addition, the biologist may be dealing with conscious material, or beings with minds, and we have only just begun to realize the interrelation between mind and body. So he has had to develop a different experimental technique, the so-called controlled experiment, where the subjects of the experiment are divided into two groups, and conditions are kept precisely the same for the two groups except for the single factor that is being examined. Then the response of one group can be compared with the response of the other and the difference in reaction can be mathematically calculated.

Of course, unlike the situation in the mathematical sciences where a single experiment can be conclusive, in the biological sciences the size of the sample is important. If the size of the sample is insufficient, the results may be affected by pure chance. In Pasteur's original demonstration of the validity of his anthrax vaccine, he used four cows, two of which were inoculated with the vaccine while the other two received none and constituted the control. The experiment worked and the two vaccinated cows remained alive and healthy while the other two sickened and died when all four were inoculated with anthrax germs. But afterward, when the vaccine became widely used, it was found that some animals grazing in infected fields developed anthrax even though they had been vaccinated and others even though not inoculated were not affected because of a natural immunity.

In the social sciences we are concerned with the minds of men and how their reactions are manifested in their behavior. In economics we focus our attention on the way they distribute their wealth, in government on how power and responsibility are divided, and in psychology on people's behavior under various conditions. Here, the problem is complicated not only because the mind is a far more intricate organ than the body, but by two other subtle considerations. First, the investigator is essentially looking at himself or at an individual like himself. He cannot stand off from his subject and view him with objectivity and detachment; he is always himself on the stage of the microscope. Second, the mere act of looking affects the thing looked at. Consider the stock market tipster who notifies his customers that a stock is going up: they rush to buy and the stock goes up, whether it is good or bad, in response to their own demand. It is the observation itself, the mere act of making it, that affects the stock. Or say a study is initiated to determine if there is a need for a special government aid to a particular group, and investigators are sent out into the field. The people who are being studied will respond in a way that they assume will produce favorable action. The results are announced and measures are adopted that are calculated to change it.

But the problem is even more complicated, for while some will try to convince the investigators that their situation is worse than it is in the hope of getting more relief and more quickly, others will be motivated by embarrassment and will minimize their condition. Even in medicine, where the concern is with the body primarily rather than the mind, the doctor finds that in taking case histories—and his patients have come willingly and are aware of the importance of giving correct information because it may be necessary for the relief of their suffering—his patients frequently minimize and exaggerate; the same patient frequently minimizes certain aspects of his condition while exaggerating others.

Indeed, even where subjects make every effort to tell the truth, their own subconscious fears and desires interfere and lead them to conceal certain aspects of their cases while they gloss over others, and in certain areas suffer either mental blocks or complete lapses of memory.

The sad fact is, of course, that the studies of government and economics and psychology and education and sociology and the rest are not really sciences at all in the sense of offering predictability; by the very nature of the material they deal with, they never will be. But they offer useful methods of examining and explaining the mistakes of the past, thereby promoting new theories on which new procedures may be developed. The present study may be regarded as just such an analysis and examination in the field of education.

Perhaps the most basic reason why the social sciences can never develop the kind of exact predictability we associate with the mathematical sciences, or even the reasonable predictability of the biological sciences, is that in the social sciences the conditions of the study or experiment are never the same twice; they can never be duplicated. The attempted repetition of an experiment or a study always involves the change in attitude of the subject and/or the experiment as a result of the first experiment. The reaction of the group to the boy who cried "Wolf" indicates this basic situation. If a different group is used, there is no certainty that it is similar to the first in all particulars; and they will also show a reaction from what they have heard of the first experiment.

As a result of such special problems, special methods and techniques are involved: the employment of large groups and statistical analysis, and the use of the questionnaire as a method of securing information. Insofar as possible, the controlled experiment is used as in the biological sciences—but with a significant difference. Because degree of predictability can be high in the biological sciences, a positive correlation is apt to be the stepping stone to further work along the same lines in the hopes of increasing the percentage of correlation. In the social sciences the correlation is likely to be the end of the study.

The most significant difference in method, however, is that the social sciences rely heavily on reason and deductive logic. An explanation of a sociological phenomenon that is logical and reasonable, that includes all elements involved and weighs them on the basis of their apparent and likely significance, is accepted as "true" in the sense that it becomes the working hypothesis for further study. Of course, one cannot always be sure that one has included all the elements and there is even less certainty that one has ascribed to them their proper significance in the problem as a whole. So another investigator, dealing with the same phenomena, can come up with an entirely different explanation, and this will also be "true," for sociological truth is a relative thing, and perhaps the term should be eschewed entirely and we should substitute for it a concept that will imply that which is honest, reasonable, thorough, and plausible.

An essential difference between mathematical and biological science on the one hand, and social science on the other is that in the former we do not really proceed on the basis of logic at all, as it is commonly understood. The fundamental principle of the mathematical and biological sciences is *post hoc, ergo propter hoc*. If one condition or situation invariably follows another condition or situation, then the first is said to be the cause of the second and the second the result of the first. But there need not be any reasonable, in the sense of rational and understandable, connection between the two. If A threatens to kill B, B may run away, or he may arm himself, or he may try to enlist the help of friends, or he may adopt a posture of defense and stand his ground, or he may himself strike a surprise blow. Whichever he does would be a logical and reasonable response to the situation and one which was demonstrably evoked by it. But there is no reason why two parts hydrogen and one part oxygen produce water, or why cutting the lines of force in a magnet with a wire produces an electric current, or why a tiny amount of a foreign protein injected in the bloodstream of a large organism is frequently fatal. They just happen. It is merely the way the physical world is organized.

We say that the mathematical sciences are based on inductive logic. And the difference between inductive and deductive logic is usually explained as the one reasoning from the particular to the general and the other from the general to the particular. The implication is that these are two roads leading to the same place. Actually, inductive logic is not really logic at all. At least it is not logical. An example will demonstrate the difference between the two far better than the above definition.

From where I am sitting I can see many houses. I cannot see their roofs, but I know they all have roofs. How do I arrive at this conclusion? Inductively, I say that I have seen thousands of houses and since they all had roofs and I have never seen a house without a roof, I can safely assume that these houses also have roofs. There is no causal relationship demonstrated and the same reasoning would apply if instead of roofs I were dealing with something like a hex symbol painted on the back door. Deductively, I arrive at the same conclusion by demonstrating that houses are weatherproofing against the elements and it is logical to assume that these have roofs since in this climate there must be protection from above as well as from the sides.

Deductive logic therefore involves demonstrably causal relationships, whereas inductive logic involves only *post hoc* and hence temporal relationships—which, to be sure, may ultimately be proved causal. In that sense research in the mathematical sciences has an accidental, serendipitous flavor, and one reason for urging basic research is precisely that. "Basic" research as opposed to planned research is frequently more successful and more productive for the very reason that discovery is a matter of chance.

Social science research, on the other hand, tends to be teleological; the investigator seeks a specific explanation for a specific series of behavioral patterns. The order in which they appear is usually known; it is in fact the reason for the investigation. What is wanted is the causal relationship between them. Thus, for example, we usually know the characteristics of a migration pattern: when young people reach a certain age, they leave the country for the city. It is apt to be common knowledge. The economist, the sociologist, and the government expert want to know why.

There is a pecking order in academic circles and the professors of the exact sciences stand at the top because of the exactness and complete predictability of their discipline. Biologists stand lower in the scale because biology does not offer 100 percent predictability and hence is felt to be less scientific. And of course, since the social sciences offer very little predictability, they stand lower still and there is some question whether they are sciences at all. This general sentiment in academic circles has no doubt affected the direction that the social sciences have taken in recent years. The social scientist has been so anxious to establish the scientific nature of his study that he has emphasized those aspects of his field that are similar to the mathematical sciences, especially measurement. The social scientist is entranced by figures and formulae and other scientific apparatus and paraphernalia, and it is a legitimate question whether this may not have contributed to the sterility of his discipline.

This difference in attitude among the practitioners of the three types of science points up the basic error, one to which most people are normally prone, that there is only one kind of truth and that is the truth capable of 100 percent demonstration. From this point of view the biological sciences are edging toward true scientific status and are now at the point where physics and chemistry were, say, in the seventeenth century. And the social sciences in this scheme of things stand in relation to the true sciences perhaps as alchemy stood to chemistry and astrology to astronomy.

When we realize, however, that each type of knowledge has its own test of truth, there is no reason for the derogation of the social sciences. They call for a different test of truth from that of the mathematical sciences because of the essential nature of the material dealt with. The chemist or physicist who views the social sciences with tolerant amusement as he might the primitive experiments in the early days of his own field has a mental blind spot. The social scientist could answer that his findings at least have the merit of being demonstrably logical, whereas those of the chemist or physicist are frequently the result of pure luck and are merely coincidental.

History is sometimes considered one of the social sciences, but in one respect at least the historian is more fortunate since his concern is with the past and he consequently is not involved with the problem of predictability. He escapes the tensions because he lacks the pretensions of the social scientist and is not in the position of trying to compete with the mathematical scientist.

In philosophy and mathematics the deductive logic that was an important factor in the social sciences and history is the basic method. Once the premises have been established, subsequent development of theory is a series of logical deductions—although the conclusions are subject to comparison with reality step to step. But the method of arriving at each successive step is logical deduction. It is a curious psychological phenomenon that scientists, who require mathematics as a tool and who accept its method without question, are apt to be contemptuous of philosophy as pilpulistic wordplay even though it makes use of the same test of truth. Recent developments in the sciences, however, have forced them to take note of the philosophical implications of their research and as a result the philosopher has acquired a new status in academic circles. At the same time, however, philosophy has developed an unfortunate tendency toward the esoteric and the arcane so that it has become almost meaningless to all except the philosophy specialist.

The greatest divergence, however, appears between the arts and the sciences. Here the difference is so great that C. P. Snow speaks of the two as representing two distinct cultures.

At times the adherents of these two great divisions of knowledge appear to be almost two races of man. The attitude of the science and/or engineering student toward literature is "But it isn't true." He cannot understand the significance of a story that is not grounded in cold, hard fact. He can understand history or biography—after all, they happened. But imaginative literature he tends to think of in much the same way that he regards the cinema; it has some value as a means of relaxation, as a way of passing an idle hour, as an escape from boredom, but hardly as something to be taken seriously.

Poetry, of course, is even worse. There his objection is "All he says is that it's a nice day." He knows about symbols—he uses them all the time in his own work—but *his* mean something definite and are the same all the time, whereas in poetry the meaning of the symbol is not clear and what meaning it has is good for this trip only.

The scientist-engineer is apt to show a greater acceptance of music and painting than he does of literature. In the visual arts, painting and sculpture, there is the quality of manual workmanship for which he can have a fine appreciation. And similarly, he can appreciate the sheer dexterity of the musical performer, the racing fingers of the pianist or the violinist, as well as having an awareness of the special quality of the vocal chords of the singer. And of course, he cannot fail to react to the rhythm of music since its appeal goes far deeper than the conscious mind. But most of all, his tolerance of music and of the visual arts—and frequently it is a little more than tolerance—is due to the fact that these arts do not make flat statements about reality, as does literature, which his mind has been conditioned to contradict if not proved according to his very special test of truth.

On the other hand, the literature student shows a corresponding condescension to the sciences. As far as the findings of the social scientists are concerned, he is in a position to point out that Shakespeare or Milton or Chaucer said it hundreds of years ago—and said it better. Of course the one is intuitive and the other is the result of investigation, but it is the conclusion that he considers important. Typical of the attitude is Chesterton's remark that half of what the social scientists claim, everyone has known all along, and the other half isn't true.

The literature/art student readily admits that the physical sciences gave us telephones and streetcars and modern plumbing and electric guitars, but since his orientation is aesthetic, he regards these as contributary—if they are—to the good life rather than the good life itself. He accepts new scientific discoveries with a kind of wonder, but once the novelty has worn off, he regards them as a matter of course, like chairs and tables. He has no appreciation or even understanding of the great beauty of a scientific theory or experiment. And since so many of the great scientific discoveries are serendipitous, he is likely to feel that no greater honor is due the discoverer than is due the man who happens to find a pocketbook in the gutter.

He is guided by a different test of truth from that of the scientist. Truth for him, in literature and in the arts, is an inner coherence that may, but need not, correspond to reality. *Alice in Wonderland* is true because it has an inner coherence. So too are the paintings of El Greco for all their unrealistically elongated figures. So is Milton's *Paradise Lost* even though it deals with Heaven and Hell and angels and devils. And the inevitability with which note follows note in a Beethoven symphony is for him proof enough that it mirrors truth.

Most literature not only has an inner coherence, but also corresponds to reality and thereby gives us another test of truth. The newspaper gives us a factual account of events that occur from day to day. But the stories have no connection with each other save that they all occurred on the previous day, so that the paper as a whole is basically meaningless. There is little discrimination as to what is included and little proportion; it is like a painting in which only what is red is depicted. Literature, however, creates a world that corresponds to the world as we know it and that has an inner coherence which presents all factors in their proper proportion and relationship to each other so that we can understand this world of the book, and, because it parallels reality, gain understanding of the real world around us.

The medium of literature is language and the nature of the medium affects what is wrought in it.

It is not that the French and the Germans have peculiar ways of saying the same things that we say so much more intelligibly in English; because their language is different, they say different things. They say different things because they have a different language; and because they have a different language, they say different things. This is the educative value of foreign-language study: it gives a kind of triangulation to our thinking.

Unfortunately, here in America, foreign-language study occupies largely an ancillary position in the curriculum. Teaching methods have changed radically in recent years and now entail a laboratory full of apparatus, tape recorders, and such to teach the language in its oral form and to ensure purity of accent. No doubt it is extremely practical, since many of our students go abroad sometime during their college careers, and those who do not, expect to go soon after. It is most helpful in communicating with waiters and bus drivers. But in this form it hardly seems like a proper subject for a liberal arts curriculum anymore than does a course in typing or shorthand, which are also extremely useful.

Nor was it any different in the old days before World War II when a trip abroad was unlikely before one had made one's pile and retired. Then, French and German were studied as reading languages much as Latin was studied, a matter of substituting an English word for a French word until the meaning became reasonably clear—the interlinear "trot" method. But although the emphasis was on the literature, it was basically ancillary in character. It was not an introduction to the French mind or the German, but chiefly a tool for reading French and German texts that were not as yet in English translation. "A reading knowledge of French and German is required"—so ran the announcement in the graduate school catalogue. It still does.

In my own experience, seven years of Latin study in high school and college did not give me either an insight into the mind of the Roman or a feeling for his language. I was required, as was the custom, to translate literally the works we were studying, substituting an English word for a Latin word with no attempt to produce idiomatic English. It was a "trot" rather than a translation, a pedestrian business of looking up each unfamiliar word in the vocabulary in back of the book, presumably to show that I had done it, an exercise in perseverance but not in translation. The accepted rendering of the common phrase *quae cum ita sint,* for example, was "which when these things were so." A few years later, in a graduate course in English, I was asked to write a translation of the first twenty or so lines of Virgil's *Aeneid,* a true translation so that the English would have the same effect on the English reader as the original had on the Roman. And only then, in the several weeks that I worked at it, did I begin to get a feeling for the genius of the Latin poet and the economy of the language he worked in.

Naturally, the subject matter of each course has its own unique lessons. Astronomy teaches not only the mathematically scientific test of truth, but also the immensity of the universe, the mind-stretching concepts of astronomical distances and magnitudes, and the order of the movement of heavenly bodies. History teaches not only the social science test of truth, but historical perspective and the logical march of events that led up to and influenced the panorama of the present. A course in literature teaches not only the artistic test of truth, but also offers in the individual works studied the best evidence of the thinking of the age that produced them, an insight into the extraordinary minds of the writers which mirrored the minds of their contemporaries, and the opportunity to study and to enjoy the soul-satisfying creations themselves.

But these are lagniappe. The essential rationale for the liberal arts curriculum is that it introduces the student to the major tests of truth and thus opens his mind to an understanding of all phenomena. In that sense, it can be said that the liberal arts curriculum takes all knowledge for its province. Whether the student remembers the details of his courses or not, he will at least have been given an understanding of the different approaches that the various aspects of reality require.

CHAPTER 5

How It Changed

Given the function of the liberal arts college as the education of the individual for his own improvement, it would follow that the instruction would have characteristics quite different from those of the professional or training school. For one thing, like the Y gym, it would be relatively easy to get into, as long as one was qualified. Obviously, some qualifications are needed just as they are to gain admission to the Y gym. The Y probably would not want to accept someone for their normal program of physical exercise if he were subject to a heart attack or a cerebral shock. So too, they might have misgivings about someone who lacked the normal complement of arms and legs. They might in all of these cases work out some special program of exercise, to be sure, but it would be understandable if the director of the program was to tell the candidate that he ought to take his exercise under a doctor's supervision and that their program was not for him.

Similarly, it is understandable that the college should require sufficient preparation on the part of the applicant to ensure his capacity to carry on the normal classwork involved in higher study. This would normally be passing grades in a stipulated program in the high school, perhaps endorsed by passing grades in a series of examinations given by people not connected with the high school, to ensure that the passing grades in the school were not the result of favoritism on the part of the teachers. If the student were not so qualified, he would be unable to derive the benefit of the courses in the college, just as the applicant with a heart condition would be unable to derive the benefit of the exercises at the Y gym.

And presumably, admission would tend to be on a first-come-first-served basis, as it is in the Y or in a hospital, or a theater, or a streetcar, or any other institution that is open to and intended for the general public.

Of course, the situation in the baseball training camp is quite different. There, it is not a matter of accepting candidates in the order of their application. Nor is it a matter of qualifying, either, but rather a matter of selection.

The manager of a professional baseball team is not satisfied with merely capable players; he wants the best that he can recruit and he will ruthlessly replace a very good player if a better one is available. Similarly, the law school, the medical school, the army and navy service schools have a right to limit their enrollments not merely to those who qualify, but to the best of those who qualify—because the training they dispense, although the student will earn his living by it, is primarily for the service of society.

The practitioners of these professions have responsibilities to the community at large and in return receive special privileges from the community. We rely on them. We rely on the doctor to cure us when we are sick; we take the medicines he prescribes on the basis of the diagnosis that he makes; and if in his opinion surgery is called for, we submit to surgery at his hands. Anyone else who would presume to diagnose and prescribe medicine, let alone practice surgery, would be liable to serious legal penalties. Similarly, we rely on the lawyer to defend us when we are in trouble—and in certain areas only he is permitted to. Although it is not stipulated by law, in practice he also frames our laws and judges us when we may have broken them. These are certainly important privileges and we accord them to the legal profession because we feel that basically the profession is practiced in our behalf and for the general good.

We take the word of the engineer that the bridge he built is safe and will not collapse. And we trust that the electrical circuitry that the electrician installed in our house will not electrocute us. That all these people make a living in the performance of these services—sometimes a very good living—is incidental. Basically, they are working for us. The doctor did not study in case he himself or his family should get sick any more than the electrician learned his trade in order to install the electricity in his own house. The one, like the other, did it for us, the community as a whole.

It is understandable, therefore, that society for its own protection try to limit the professions to the best students only. It is comforting when you are sick to know that the physician who is treating you has not only received the best possible training, but that, as a specially selected student, he was best able to profit from the training offered him.

So we see some logic in the careful selection of candidates for admission to the law school and the medical school and the army and navy academies even though the best medical student does not always make the best doctor. Indeed, a recent survey of medical school graduates of a dozen years ago showed that it was the B student rather than the A student who reached the top of his profession. We will consider the possible reasons for this later on, but for the present let us grant that it is reasonable at least to try to select the best students for the professions. But is there any point in trying to get the very best students for the liberal arts college when its function does not involve the service of the public but is intended solely for the student himself?

If the college of liberal arts does adopt the admissions philosophy of the professional school, then it is a fair assumption that from the point of view of its administrators its function has changed. It is as though a Y director instituted a policy of turning down the flabby and the potbellied and began to restrict admissions to the gymnasium program to athletes with rippling muscles. Obviously, the suspicion would arise that he was not so much interested in the physical improvement of his members for their own good, but rather that he was out to make a showing of some kind, to win the inter-Y track meet, perhaps, or the state Y basketball tournament. And although he might be congratulated by his superior and be given a silken banner to display proudly in the lobby or a silver cup for his trophy cabinet, he would nevertheless have perverted the purpose of his institution and changed it to something quite different.

Similarly, when the liberal arts college makes its selections not on the basis of whether the applicant is qualified, but rather on the basis of accepting those with the highest marks they can attract, the suspicion grows that the function of the college has been perverted, that it is no longer what it was, and that it has become—in spite of the nature of its curriculum—another professional school.

Other aspects of the college suggest that the suspicion is well founded. A famous English educator surveying the American college scene expressed his surprise at the amount of work required of the student. To him it seemed that the American student was being stuffed and crammed with information like a Strasbourg goose. He suggested that the American professor regards his students as so many empty pails which it is his job to fill, whereas the traditional view is that the student is tinder which the professor hopes to set aflame.

In studying for a profession, the more information the student can absorb, the better. It is useful information that can conceivably come in handy someday to the benefit of the patient or the client. If remembered, the obscure symptoms that suggest the rare disease can lead to diagnosis and cure. The little-known judicial ruling can win a case. Teaching that increases the student's store of knowledge is proper and reasonable in professional training. But the purpose of liberal arts education is not so much to increase the student's store of knowledge as to increase his understanding. Evolving an original theory even if it is subsequently seen to be untenable is better for his mental development than committing to memory a carefully thought out theory that his teacher propounds.

Like the situation that obtains at the baseball training camp, the professional school is highly competitive. Understandably so. The student stands at the threshold of a career where he will be competing for the favor of the public he has undertaken to serve. The lawyer is in competition with all other lawyers and the doctor with his fellow doctors. There are desirable positions and perquisites to be fought for. As a student, his class standing will determine not only whether he will make *Law Review* but what jobs will be offered him on graduation. He is embarking on a career in a competitive society. Like the professional baseball player he has to show a competitive spirit to make the team, because the team is engaged in competition.

Unfortunately, the same spirit of competition has developed in the liberal arts college, but hardly with the same justification. A fat man who joins the Y gym to reduce may compete at the scales with others in the same class, but it is good-natured competition intended to urge each other on. He has joined in order to derive a personal benefit. If he feels better as a result of losing weight, then he has been successful. Why should he care if someone else has lost more? But the competition in the liberal arts college these days is obviously not of that nature; it is cutthroat.

It manifests itself in the rise of cheating that has been observed in colleges throughout the country. Some estimates have run as high as 50 percent of the student body. Cheating was not unknown in college in my own day, but there was a difference.

Forty years ago, when the college was still a college of liberal arts, weak students who had played too much and studied too little occasionally panicked before examinations and resorted to cheating in an effort to remain in college. But cheating today is observed among high-ranking students, and the purpose is not to remain in college. This would be understandable. But they are in no danger of failing. The purpose nowadays is to surpass one's fellows, with whom one is in competition.

Again, the teaching in the professional school is essentially quantitative and relevant. The more the law student knows about his profession, the better he can function as a lawyer. And if his knowledge is not relevant to the modern situation, it is useless to him. But the very idea of liberal education is that not quantitative knowledge but understanding is important. And the essence of a liberal education is that *everything* is relevant.

Why then has the liberal arts college adopted professional-school methods and characteristics? A clue may be found in the number who go on to graduate study. In the prestige colleges, as many as 90 percent of the graduates go on to graduate study—suggesting that the A.B. degree is no longer regarded as terminal. It has become a mere breathing place on the road to the professional degree. In effect, it has become an adjunct of the professional school, a part of it, with the same pedagogical philosophy.

The fact is, in America the liberal arts college has practically ceased to exist as a separate institution with a separate function.

CHAPTER 6

What Caused the Change

Although the change became manifest in the early forties, there were already signs in the thirties, during the great Depression. Prior to the Depression, in the prosperous twenties, presidents of smaller colleges had beaten the bushes urging the liberal arts college. Their argument was largely economic, that it increased earning power. Of course, they did not usually bother to point out that college students also represented a higher economic group with greater opportunities for getting good jobs and for promotion afterwards, and for that reason they would probably show greater earning capacity even if they had never gone to college.

It is hard to estimate how effective the sales pitch was. On the admittedly shaky basis of my own recollection, it had little influence in deciding the young high school senior to apply for admission to college rather than to get a job. Those who elected college usually did so for other reasons: because they did not want to go to work as yet; because it sounded like fun; because there was an opportunity to make valuable contacts; and, most of all, because they had a greater desire to learn than to earn. Perhaps they used the last as a rationalization in discussion with their fellows or even as a means of persuading their parents to undertake the additional expense.

But curiously enough, it was in the Depression, when fewer could afford to go, and when the smaller and less solvent colleges were actually having difficulty in keeping their doors open, that the college presidents' argument began to take hold.

Because jobs were so scarce, college men competed for any that were available: stock boy at twelve dollars a week for a sixty- to seventy-hour week, office boy at ten dollars a week, elevator operator, house-to-house canvasser, even busboy at six to eight dollars a week and meals. And they were given preference over high school graduates, either because they were four years older or, more likely, on the general principle that if you are offered a Ford and Cadillac at the same price, you will naturally choose the Cadillac. Perhaps the employer—himself, as he was fond of saying, a graduate of the College of Hard Knocks—liked the idea of a college graduate working under him and in the most humble capacity.

When the federal government under the Roosevelt administration began to recruit in vast numbers for the make-work projects that were the American alternative to the charity dole, the higher positions, supervisory and administrative, and better paying, were allotted to those with the better education; few of those on the projects had had any work experience, so it was the only way to differentiate.

Again, when America entered the war, the college man received preferential treatment. The high school graduate was drafted into the army as a private; the college man through the R.O.T.C. and Officers Candidate School could go in as an officer. After the war, the large corporations that were taking an ever-increasing share of the nation's business adopted the same rigid stratification that obtained in the armed services. Just as the enlisted man could work up to master sergeant—and no more—so the young high school graduate who started in industry in an overall or blue collar job could only become a straw boss or a storekeeper, whereas the college man was accepted in the executive training program.

The net effect over the years of the Depression, and in the war years that followed, was to establish a close connection in the minds of the public at large between a college degree on the one hand and preferential treatment and economic advancement on the other. College was no longer a place where the rich man's son spent four years in play as a preliminary to buckling down to a job in his father's business—a kind of last kicking up the heels of freedom before assuming the harness; nor was it merely the necessary preliminary screening and testing for those planning to go on to one of the professional schools. Nor was it even the place that gave you a little extra something that enabled you to earn more during your lifetime as the college presidents had said in their phony pitch. It was much more serious. In the minds of the general public, it was now the *sine qua non* for practically any white collar job that had a chance of leading anywhere. If you were satisfied with a lifetime of pumping gas at a filling station—fine. But if you wanted something that carried a higher social status and the opportunity for a decent salary, then you had to go to college.

This change in the public attitude toward the college made it a different kind of institution. Collegiate study had been purely optional; now it was almost compulsory. Formerly, one could go or not go and, if one chose not to go, there were no sanctions imposed by society. Now, not to have a degree of some sort was to start off with a severe handicap, one that conceivably limited the social and economic levels to which the young man could aspire.

With college a necessity, there was naturally a tremendous increase in the number of students seeking admission. The increase was astronomical. It was no longer necessary for college presidents to sell the idea that college would improve one's lifetime earnings. It was now clear that if you were to have any sort of career at all, you would need a college degree.

This was an important crossroad in the history of the college of liberal arts. And the colleges took the wrong road!

The size of the student bodies of most private colleges had been more or less set before the Depression began. As the demand for admission increased, the colleges instead of increasing their facilities chose rather to increase the standard of admission. Thus Harvard, for example, had set its freshman class at a thousand back in the late twenties because this represented what might be called their normal rate of admission. To be sure, every year they received more than a thousand applicants, but after subtracting those who were unable to meet the entrance requirements, and those who could not afford the financial burden, and those who in the end decided to go elsewhere, the figure usually salted down to a thousand. As the number of applications increased to two thousand they still accepted only a thousand, taking the top half; when it increased to three thousand, the top third; when it reached ten thousand, the top tenth. And this has remained the policy down to the present day when the number of applications could very well be in the hundreds of thousands.*

You have openings for ten salesmen in your organization and twenty apply, you take the ten best. If you can afford to wait and a hundred or two hundred apply, it is worthwhile going to considerable trouble to get the ten best. Why take a good salesman when you can get a very good one? Or a very good one when

---

* The Admissions Department at Harvard claims that the most they receive in any one year is ten thousand applications rather than the several hundred thousand claimed above. This is an artificial figure, however. Prestige in the college has become more and more important from year to year, and Harvard is perhaps the most prestigious university in the country today. The reason that the applications do not run much more than ten thousand is that all high schools now have guidance counselors who lead their students away from the colleges where they are

you can get a sales genius? It is the system followed by the baseball training camps, and even more by the teams that are strictly limited as to number by league regulations.

On the other hand, a theater also has just so many seats. But when the play is popular and the demand for tickets is great, no attempt at selection is made. There is no attempt to parcel out the tickets to those who are apt to be the most appreciative.

Of course, if the demand for play tickets is great, the producer might extend the play's run or move the play to a larger theater. So too, airlines, like railroads, add sections, when possible, to meet increased demand. If the colleges had similarly expanded their facilities to keep pace with the demand, higher education might not have changed its direction.

Some colleges, notably the state colleges, did expand, since in most cases they were committed by law to admitting all the graduates of their high schools. There were also a number of small colleges with little in the way of endowment funds that were almost entirely dependent on tuition fees and that had been struggling for their very existence since their founding. They took this increase in available business as a golden opportunity to expand. And, of course, a number of new colleges were founded since the pressure for admission guaranteed not only their ability to survive, but even their prosperity.

But by and large, the prestigious private foundations kept the size of their enrollments at the same level as it had been during the Depression, and used the opportunity offered by the great increase in number of applicants to raise the level of their student body.

---

unlikely to find admission. Hence there is a preliminary selection of students, and only those with the very best academic records and grades in the College Board examinations bother to make application to Harvard at all. If it were not for this artificial limitation, as well as the less formal limitation resulting from the common knowledge that the college takes only the top 1 or 2 percent of those seeking admission, the number would be easily ten or twenty times the number who actually make formal application.

To the old grad of the prestige college revisiting his alma mater after an absence of ten or twenty years, for commencement exercises perhaps, phenomenal growth seems to have taken place. The campus has been enlarged and there are scores of new buildings, but as the academic procession files by, he realizes that the liberal arts student body is not much, if any, larger than in his own day. The new buildings are dormitories, laboratories, recreation halls, special libraries, but they serve no more undergraduate students than attended years ago.

With far more applicants than places available, it seemed altogether normal to take those with the best academic records. With two thousand applicants for one thousand places, it was normal, natural, and logical to take the thousand best. Why take a C student when you could get an A student? It is the old Ford–Cadillac situation again.

But what to do when all the applicants are A students? When the number of applicants increased to ten thousand for the same thousand places, it was no longer a choice between a C student and an A student, but a choice between one A student and another. The A, of course, represents a range of achievement—say, in a numerical scale of 100, the range from 90 to 100. In keeping with the principle, a 99A would be better than a mere 90A. So what was needed was a marking system that could be more finely tuned than the old five-letter system of A to F.

This was not a simple matter of notifying secondary schools to report their students' grades numerically on the scale of 100 rather than by the letter system. The marking system depends on the testing system. If the testing system calls for essay-type answers because the teaching method involves the understanding of concepts, then the marking system has to be comparatively loose. Judging an essay is first of all highly subjective. An essay will have one impact on one examiner and quite another on someone else. It can even have a different impact on the same examiner if he reads it at a different time. But more, how do you weigh the relative merits of a bright, original thought, albeit poorly expressed, against a common idea well expressed? How much value do you place on mechanical accuracy? How much credit do you deduct for a mistake in spelling or punctuation? How much for an obvious slip and how much for an error due to ignorance? Obviously, a system of essay-type testing calls for a loose grading system like the letter system.

So to make use of a finely tuned system requires a different method of marking, which requires a different method of testing. Fortunately, psychologists had been working in a related field—to develop a test for general intelligence—and educators were able to take advantage of their spadework to develop the "objective test."

But what is the validity of the objective test on which so much of our present-day educational practice depends? And how did it influence the change in the liberal arts idea and ideal that led ultimately to the student rebellions and campus riots?

CHAPTER 7

Tests—of What?

There is, as indicated earlier, a vast chasm between the more exact sciences on the one hand and the so-called social sciences on the other. It is not merely the slight difference that separates the mathematical sciences and the biological sciences because of the difference in the type of material dealt with; it is rather a difference of approach, method, and result.

But because the practitioners of the more exact sciences are the darlings of the twentieth century, the social scientists have been trying to jump aboard the bandwagon and to appear as part of the same apparatus that has given us the modern miracles of electricity, plastics, and vaccines. The papers in their learned journals bristle with figures and mathematical equations. They cultivate a scientific jargon and conceal simple and common concepts by substituting esoteric phrases for the well-known words.

Since the exact sciences are basically a matter of measurement, the social scientist likewise concentrates on measuring things.

In World War I, the army was faced with the problem of training large groups of men in the special techniques that modern warfare required—from telegraphy and motor mechanics to cooking and baking. How to find the relatively few, the thousands, capable of learning these techniques quickly, from the hundreds of thousands and millions of draftees who were available? Here is a contingent of ten thousand men. The vast majority of them would become infantrymen, doughboys. But five hundred perhaps were required for special training to fill the technical jobs that the army needed done. So the Army Alpha Intelligence Test was developed. It permitted a quick sorting that could be done by a clerk with little or no special knowledge or training. It was not an exact test, by any means. But the feeling was that if the test accidentally included in the superior group a few who later showed that they lacked the capacity to learn the special technique or skill for which they had been chosen, they could easily be washed out. And if by chance the army had overlooked some who might have had special skills but became infantrymen, no great harm would be done. The army was not concerned with individuals but with large groups.

From these modest beginnings, psychologists, intoxicated by the ready acceptance of the method, have proceeded to measure all kinds of personal characteristics, with increasingly bold asseverations of exactness and accuracy. And they have never looked back. The psychological test has become a way of life with us and it is rarely questioned.

For schools they measure not only the intelligence of their students—the tests quickly received the same acceptance good Catholics accord to the *ex cathedra* pronouncements of the Pope—but the capacity of the student to pursue courses that he had not as yet studied. And this, not in a loose general sort of way—pass or fail, or good, or average, or below average—but on a curve with individual mathematical values in which 97 is higher than 96 just as it is in counting.

For industry, they measure the capacities of applicants for specific jobs; for management they measure the leadership potential of executives and their ability to integrate with the team; for business, they measure the appeal of a new product to the buying public.

In the press and in popular magazines, questionnaires are constantly being published that enable the reader to test and evaluate himself—the degree of his extroversion or introversion, his capacity for friendship, his capacity for love, his success as a husband, the accuracy of his judgment, his sensitivity, his memory, his capacity to make decisions, his general knowledge, his wisdom, his liberalism, his open-mindedness, his—almost anything! And ours being a competitive society, we go on to establish a marking system to pick the best of the category.

We not only pick the ten best-dressed men and the ten best-dressed women every year but we then go on to assign each of them a rank in the ten. We pick the athlete of the year and the secretary of the year, and even the mother of the year.

Every year we pick Miss America and we pick her not only for her beauty, but for her talent and charm and poise and personality, all of which go into the scoring system. From the fifty winners in the contests in the fifty states, fifteen semifinalists are selected; and from these, five finalists are in turn selected—the five of the fifteen of the fifty of the hundred million. Excitement mounts as the fifth most beautiful, most talented, most poised, most personable is named. And then the fourth and the third. When there are only two left excitement and tension reach fever pitch. The toothy master of ceremonies names the second etcetera, etcetera and there is a wild burst of applause as the new Miss America buries her face in her hands, her poise momentarily deserting her in the flood of her emotion.

Of course, much of it is just fun and games. The Secretary of the Year is a popular girl whose friends at the annual secretarial convention have campaigned for her. And the Athlete of the Year is not the best athlete—how can you compare golfers and tennis players and prize fighters?—but the one who has received the most press coverage. But for the great mass of Americans, although there may be disagreement with the final choice, there is no dispute with the basic concept. There is no thought that there are some things that cannot be measured and hence cannot be ranked. They see nothing absurd in the concept of the Best Baseball Player, and the second best and the third best and so on, or the Best Football Player, or the Best College or the Best Restaurant. And the theory and practice of modern psychology supports them in this nonsense.

Let us be very clear about it because it is of great importance. The best tennis player, the best golfer, the best chess player—these are reasonable and logical concepts because in each case the champion's superiority over all rivals has been demonstrated by beating them. But the best baseball player is an illogicality, a meaningless nonconcept, because there is no and can be no method of demonstrating the superiority. The one is legitimate fact; the other just public relations fun and games.

Or consider the difference between the Miss America contest on the one hand and a dog show on the other. In the former a group of ten or a dozen judges, male and female—chosen God knows how or why—each with different ideas of what constitutes beauty, poise, personality, and talent, grade the fifty contestants on the basis of these attributes, and the one who scores the highest number of votes is declared the winner.

In the dog show on the other hand, one man, an accepted expert, judges all the dogs in a single breed. He has in his mind an image of the perfect example of the breed—the Platonic prototype, of the poodle or spaniel or airedale—and he measures each dog in turn against the same yardstick, the image in his mind, the classic model. The one that comes closest to this ideal image is declared the champion. Probably the perfect specimen does not actually exist and every winner is to some extent a compromise. When the field has been narrowed down to two or three, the judge may have to decide whether the less than perfect formation of the ears of one dog is a greater flaw, a more significant disparity with the ideal, than is the less than perfect droop of the tail of the competing animal. But they are both matched against the same mental image. What is more, the breed itself is a man-made concept. The breed was developed by men who endowed it with specific characteristics. It is an artificial contrivance which dogs themselves are not party to and have no understanding of. Dogs play together and breed indiscriminately. There is no evidence that a beagle prefers another beagle to a poodle, or that the champion of the class has a greater attraction for other dogs than do any other members of the breed. In establishing the breed, very specific characteristics were formulated, quite arbitrarily: no more than so many inches and no less than so many inches at the shoulder: the tail must droop, or it must curl, or even kink; the hair must be long and straight, or short and curly; these colors are acceptable and those are not. The characteristics do not always necessarily have any demonstrable relationship to the special function of the breed. If the specifications call for a curl in a completely useless tail, then a straight and equally useless tail is a fault.

The point is that in judging dogs, man is judging, godlike, his own creation. He is not concerned with the dog's opinion, only with how closely the dog conforms to his ideas of what it should look like. And the characteristics that he looks for are those on which all experts in the breed are agreed. In judging people, however, everyone is his own expert, and there is no agreement, certainly no universal agreement, on what is good and what is bad. If most Americans find Miss America at least not unattractive, Orientals may on the other hand find her features too heavy, just as we might find the features of a Chinese beauty too bland. And a Ubangi would probably consider Miss America thin-lipped to the point of deformity.

There *are* certain characteristics of people that we *can* measure objectively and accurately. We can measure physical characteristics like height and weight and lifting capacity and special types of speed and endurance. And because we can measure these characteristics objectively and accurately we can arrange a group of people in a graduated scale with respect to any one of them. Any group of people can be arranged on a graduated order with respect to height or weight or the speed with which they can run a hundred yards or the size of a weight that they can lift or the distance they can run.

As soon as we move away from the measurement of a single measurable characteristic, however, we get into trouble. We are safe as long as we restrict ourselves to what can be measured by yardstick, scale, and stopwatch. We get into trouble when the matter of judgment enters in. Even in these purely physical tests we must be sure not to adduce general capacity where we are testing only a single, individual proficiency. We can grade people accurately on a graduated scale on the speed with which they run the fifty-yard dash, but we must be careful not to confuse this with the general category of speed, for the winner of the fifty-yard dash may be slow in a mile run and he might not even be able to finish a twenty-six-mile marathon. So, too, the man who is first in lifting a heavy weight with his back may not be able to strike a hard blow with his fist. And certainly there is no correlation between being able to lift a heavy weight and throwing a baseball or stroking a golf ball or running or jumping.

So that even in a relatively comprehensible attribute like strength there is so much disagreement as to what strength consists of that comparison between individuals, except in the most general way, is impossible. How do you compare the strength required to lift a heavy weight with the strength required to propel one's body through the air in the broad jump, or that in turn with the strength required to lift one's body against the force of gravity in the high jump, or any of these in turn with the strength required to run a long distance?

Or consider the concept of health. Does it imply strength and if so, which of the above is involved? Or does it imply resistance to disease, or vitality as manifested in a general feeling of well-being, or longevity?

And yet both concepts, strength and health, have a meaning for all of us, as do beauty and talent and poise and personality. Yes, and even being well dressed and being a good mother or a good secretary. Although there cannot be universal and unanimous agreement about any of these, there can be a general and meaningful consensus. We can say this one is completely impossible as a secretary, whereas that one is acceptable and another is perhaps even exceptional. In the same way we can distinguish between the talented, the untalented, and the person of exceptional talent. Or we can agree that one girl is plain to the point of ugliness while another is a beauty and a third, while no beauty, is attractive or not unattractive.

But that is all! Because one can distinguish between the adequate and the inadequate does not mean that one can arrange a large group in a graduated order from the worst to the best. It is a cardinal rule of mensuration as well as an obvious rule of logic that one cannot measure to a greater degree of accuracy than the accuracy of the measuring device. Now the measuring device in these matters is the *consensus* of general opinion, and this is so loose a measuring device that it is questionable whether we are justified in establishing as many as three categories—inadequate, adequate, and exceptional—and whether it would not be more reasonable to limit ourselves to two: pass or fail, acceptable or inadequate.

It would appear to be fairly obvious that those human characteristics that relate to the mind are more difficult to estimate and understand, much less to measure, than are those that are purely physical. For that matter, we tend to overlook the effect of the mind on those aspects of man that we regard as purely physical. But certainly such tests of physical strength and endurance as weight lifting, wrestling, boxing, sprinting, jumping, running, involve a large share of mental effort. Certainly, the champion in any sport is not always the one whose musculature is demonstrably best adapted to the requirements of that sport. The race is not always won by the competitor whose leg muscles are best for speed; sometimes it is the degree of concentration, the intensity of desire, the stubbornness of will that determines the winner. Even facial beauty, which at first sight may seem primarily a matter of regularity and fineness of feature, will on reflection be seen as involving the effect of the mind as it manifests itself in the expression of the face. An expressionless face, a face without vivacity or charm or indication of intelligence, is a death mask.

Curiously enough, while we think of physical activity as extremely varied and would think it absurd to make comparison between a high jumper and a weight lifter, we have no hesitancy in lumping all faculties of the mind together and calling it intelligence. And our psychologists whose study of the subject should presumably have led them to a more sophisticated discrimination of the varied faculties of the mind are precisely the ones who have urged the concept and have then gone on to insist that it can be measured with great exactness.

The fault is in part semantic. Since we use the verb "to think" for any and all mental activity, we tend to regard all mental activity as essentially an exercise of the one faculty and hence the same. Consider the following:

1. "I think his name is Smith."
2. "I think I'll order the blue plate special."
3. "I think Joe will be more apt to cooperate with the rest of the group than Bill."
4. "I think his early work is more honest than his later work."
5. "I think we can get the necessary reciprocal action by using a cam."
6. "I think I'd go around the world if this deal goes through and I make a million dollars."
7. "I think the Republican Party is probably right because a better class of people belong to it."
8. "I think the A is still a little sharp."
9. "I think it needs salt."
10. "I think there's a smell of almonds in the room."

We could go on almost indefinitely, but the examples above will suffice. The first sentence indicates the memory process. It refers to memory of people and presumably association of face and name. Association of this sort is a faculty that police detectives probably have to a great degree, since it is important in their work and they are likely to improve their natural capacity for it consciously or subconsciously because it is useful to them. Other people may show a special aptitude for remembering dates, others for remembering what they have read, or heard, or seen;

still others for remembering tastes and smells—one thinks of Swann's madeleines and tea. A matter of constant amazement to me is the capacity of baseball enthusiasts to remember the seemingly unending stream of statistics generated by the sport. And again, as one who plays cards only on rare occasions, I can admire but not compete with those who remember every card that is played and by whom. Those who are adept at cards are said to have card sense, which seems to be a combination of the special memory involved in conjunction with a capacity for lightning calculation of the odds and seemingly an almost extrasensory ability to predict what their opponent will play in a given situation. I suspect that if a special study were made of the subject there would be a number of additional mental aspects that would enter into the sum total. The knack of controlling one's facial expression so as to give no clue to what one holds in one's own hand, or in dissimulation to give the wrong clue, suggests itself as one possibility. No doubt there are others.

The second sentence refers to the decision-making faculty. The distinction between line and staff, between the doers and the advisers, as fundamental in the army and even in large corporate business is predicated on the assumption that this faculty of decision making does not exist to the same extent in all men. Some can make decisions and some, like the proverbial jackass equidistant between two bales of hay, go through agony before they can make up their minds on the simplest issue. It is a matter of common experience that the capacity to make quick decisions shows no correlation with other kinds of intelligence.

Nor does it have any necessary connection with the kind of intelligence implicit in the third sentence: a special sensitivity to other people so that one can make predictions as to their behavior. Obviously, this aspect of intelligence is not a simple function of the mind but rather a complex of many mental functions. No doubt, it involves the ability to observe all but unnoticeable facial expressions, and perhaps tonal qualities in the voice, the ability to associate them with similar expressions observed and remembered, and their significance. Children are thought to have a special talent in this type of intelligence. This may well be so and, if it is, it could be because they are more apt to focus their attention not on what is said—which may be beyond their understanding—but on how it is said. And this suggests that certain mental traits can operate only when other mental traits are suppressed, like flexor and tensor muscles that cannot both be exercised at the same time.

It is unnecessary to make lengthy analyses of the traits suggested and implied in the remainder of the sentences. The next one is obviously critical judgment, which is quite different from the following one which suggests creative intelligence—in this case, mechanical creativity, it should be noted. Then follow the daydream and then rationalization, both of which are useful on occasion and yet on other occasions hamper other modes of thought. The last three sentences obviously refer to sensitivity and discrimination in three of the five senses.

The ten sentences are intended of course only as a sampling, a small sampling of the many functions of the mind. It would be no great task to list a hundred. We use the word "thought" in connection with all of them just as we use the word "work" in connection with the myriads of ways in which man earns a living. But even these few serve to point up the absurdity of regarding the mind as a simple organ with a single function that can be measured with great accuracy on the basis of a small battery of tests lasting two or three hours.

The fact is, to say that Miss Maine is the twenty-sixth most beautiful, talented, poised girl in the fifty competing and hence is more beautiful, talented etcetera than Miss Kentucky who is twenty-seventh, but not as beautiful etcetera as Miss North Dakota who is twenty-fifth is not merely unfair, but illogical and meaningless; and yet no more so than to say that Geoffrey Fistermeir has a greater verbal facility than Horst Wessel because he scored two points higher in the College Board Verbal exam. It is simply not true. And if it is not true, then the system has no more validity than a lottery. The difference is, however, that in a lottery there is no pretense that the winner is the most deserving, whereas in the test situation the pretense is that he is.

CHAPTER 8

The Admission System

The college is not a collection of buildings, but rather the people who comprise it, faculty and students. The faculty are the permanent establishment; the student body, renewing itself from year to year, is its reason for being. Each year, a class graduates and a new one comes in. Eventually, after years, some few come back to become members of the faculty. Obviously, the character of the student body depends on how it is selected. So, ultimately, does the character of the faculty since they are drawn from the student bodies of earlier years.

The director of admissions and the admissions committee are not new; they had them forty years ago. But their duties then could not have been arduous. The school janitor could have performed them for 90 percent of the applicants. The ticket taker at the theater might be said to be the director of admissions for the theater in the sense that these functions were performed for the college. The college, for all practical purposes, had room for all who applied so that there was no problem of selection. Like the ticket taker whose job is to scrutinize the tickets that are handed him to make sure that they are not counterfeit and that they are indeed for that performance, the function of the admissions committee was to determine if the applicant had taken the required courses and could give evidence of having passed them.

For the majority of applicants the job of the committee was perfunctory, a matter of checking courses taken and totaling units. But then there were the problem cases, those whose marks were on the borderline and whose passing grades were suspect and might have been a gift from a softhearted teacher or examiner; graduates of progressive schools where the curriculum was not divided into convenient units; students who showed phenomenally high marks in one major subject and yet had failed in another; not to mention the applicant whose marks were below par but whose father was an illustrious alumnus from whom the school might have expectations; or the applicant whose scholastic record left much to be desired, but who was an excellent athlete. Here judgment was involved, and the committee had to have the confidence of the college, for their decisions in a sense affected the direction and the educational policy of the institution.

But it was all open and aboveboard. In the great majority of cases the decision of the committee was predictable. If the decision was adverse, it was no crime to question them, and they were prepared to defend their position. Conceivably, they might even have changed it on occasion.

The whole business was decided on the basis of the record. There was no personal interview required or suggested. It is doubtful if they could have found time for it. I do not recall that a photograph was required to accompany the application form. Certainly there was no place on it for an essay in which one was required to explain his philosophy of life, or why he wanted to go to Prestige U., or to prove that he had qualities of leadership.

Dartmouth *did* require a personal interview for all candidates for admission. It was not with a member of the admissions committee, but with a stipulated Dartmouth alumnus living in the same area as the candidate. The story was that Dartmouth wanted to develop a type, the Dartmouth type. According to the prevailing scuttlebutt the type was the well-rounded, fresh, eager personable American boy. Conceivably, a well-rounded, fresh, eager personable American boy whose marks were low might be accepted, although perhaps low grades would indicate that he was not well rounded. Or conversely, a student with high grades who was, however, not well rounded, etcetera, might be refused. Only one of my classmates in high school went to Dartmouth. It seemed to me that he was none of these things, so either they did not apply the policy strictly, or he was able to conceal his true character from the alumnus who interviewed him.

This system of admissions obtained as long as the number of applicants was roughly equal to the number the school was prepared to admit. But then, as the number of applicants began to increase beyond the capacity of the school, the admissions committee found itself in the position to pick and choose. The state colleges, bound by law to accept all graduates of state secondary schools who qualified, and yet in spite of constant expansion never quite large enough to take all who applied, made their selections partly on the basis of when they received the applications; that is, all applications that were received by a certain date were processed, and if these did not fill the rolls, another date was established and another. Although they may have made some selection in each series, better applications in a subsequent series did not replace those already accepted.

The private prestige colleges on the other hand which were under no legal restraint and able to set their own rules used the opportunity to make the best selection they could. Why bother to take applicants who merely passed when they could fill the rolls with those who passed with honors?

But when all who passed with honors were still more than the college was prepared to admit? Here the College Board Association came to the rescue with the "objective test," an offshoot of the intelligence test developed by the psychologists.

The old tests had been of the traditional type, that is, a set of questions to be answered in essay form. And these carried a standard passing grade. The new exams are graded on a scale of 800 and have no passing grade. The questions are largely of the type in which several possible answers are given and the student selects one, which he indicates with a penciled mark. He can get the right answer by a lucky guess and he can get the right answer by a process of elimination, from having a general sense of what it is not. So in a sense the student gets credit for his partial knowledge. On the other hand, if he has an exact knowledge of the subject of the question, he can conceivably be thrown off the right answer.

I am not concerned with the relative diagnostic merits of the two types of examination—only with their effect on the admission system. Each has advantages and disadvantages. The new type has one great advantage, however: it can be graded by machine. In that sense it is indeed objective. The old type required the services of a corps of graders, and within limits they had to exercise judgment. High school and college teachers were used and it offered a welcome addition to their regular teaching salaries. There is a rumor to the effect that one can beat the system in the new type of examination by marking all the available places, but this is probably a canard. They sprout at exam time like weeds after a summer rain.

The mark in the new exam is arrived at mathematically on the basis of the number of questions answered correctly minus the number answered wrongly. It is an absolute, uncompromising mark like 642 and gives the impression that the recipient knows more about the subject than someone who received 641—which is nonsense, of course, but which nevertheless permits the college to make fine, albeit meaningless, distinctions between one candidate and another.

The candidate is also informed what percentage of examinees got a higher grade than he did. But both marks are useless to the candidate as far as enabling him to determine if he will be admitted since there is no way of knowing what the college will require in the way of grades. He cannot say, "I passed; I am qualified; admit me." There is no passing grade. Now, he can only say, "I have scored the grade of 641, which is higher than the grades of 70 percent of those who took the exam." To which the answer can be, "Yes, but 30 percent of those who took it scored higher than you." This marking system implies that the student is competing rather than proving that he is qualified. Conceivably, although it is highly unlikely, the marks for a given exam could be so low as to suggest that no one was really qualified, but it would make no difference; some would be higher than others.

In the old system, the candidate knew where he stood. The purpose of the examination was to show that he had done and understood the work, that he was therefore qualified to take the collegiate course that presumed this knowledge. The new system, while it appeared to give the college authorities a more carefully delineated profile of the applicant's abilities, prevented the candidate from knowing where he stood and what his chances of admission were. There was no passing grade—only a mark relative to the thousands of other candidates throughout the country. Oh, there were rumors—that X College required grades in the high 600s, or that Prestige U. had upped their requirements since last year and was now accepting only candidates with grades in the 700s. But they were only rumors, and no one could say for certain. All you could do was to apply to a bunch of schools and sweat it out until you heard.

The new grading system gave the admissions committees almost complete freedom of selection. But there are mechanisms that have been built into the system that insure it. There is, for example, the application form itself. It differs with different schools, to be sure, but almost all ask for one or more essays on such subjects as "Why do you want to go to college?" or

"Describe your special interests and activities," "What qualities of leadership do you feel you have and what have you done to develop them?"

It is not that these are hard to write. As a matter of fact, they are usually written with the help or advice of older members of the family. It is that they offer another basis on which one is presumably being judged. And of course there is no knowing what the Admissions Committee will consider desirable. If you say the wrong thing, will it counterbalance and negate the good showing you made in the exams? But what *is* the right thing to say? "Shall I mention that I had a newspaper route?"

"Well, it shows enterprise and initiative. I would."

"Yeah, but my grades weren't so good that year. Maybe they'll think I shouldn't have."

"And what will they think of my school grades? My math marks in my junior year weren't so hot—that Miss Jones . . ."

"Well, according to your guidance counselor, they don't go so much by the particular grades. What they want to see is if you improved. Sometimes they're more interested in someone who got a low mark in the earlier grades and boosted it up later on than someone who got good grades all along."

Where no one knows for certain about anything, rumor takes over and the one who speaks with an air of assurance becomes the expert. This is the guidance counselor who surveys the student's school grades, matches them against his scores in the College Board exam, estimates the student's qualities of leadership on the basis of his extracurricular activities, making adjustments on his appearance and personality which he judges on the basis of a twenty-minute interview, and then from the depths of his understanding and experience suggests half a dozen colleges at which the student has a chance of admission, always making certain to urge a "fall-back" school, i.e., a school in which admission is certain. And if none of them admits you, there is no one you can sue—certainly not the guidance counselor who, like a councilor-at-law, does not guarantee results.

There is also the matter of the personal interview which most colleges urge and some require. Candidates themselves tend to place great reliance on the personal interview, certain that their charm or their sincerity or whatever quality or trait of personality they pride themselves on will somehow counterbalance poor or mediocre grades.

Since it is a committee that decides, and since it is an individual who conducts the interview with the applicant, I have been much bemused by the problem of how the impressions of one interviewer are equated to those only of another. No such problems bother the candidate, however. He is concerned only with what "they" want and is determined to give it to them to the best of his ability during the interview.

I once discussed the matter with a couple of young candidates. "What do you suppose is the purpose of the interview?" I asked. "It lasts less than a half hour. The chances are that you're worried or frightened or at least ill at ease. What can they find out about you with any certainty that is not better shown in your grades?"

"Why, naturally they want to see what you look like, how you're dressed and if you make a nice appearance," one of them said with the self-satisfaction of knowing that *he* was well dressed and made a nice appearance. And his friend nodded in agreement.

"But everyone coming for an interview is going to be properly dressed and will make sure his hair is combed and his fingernails clean and trimmed," I urged.

"You kidding? Take Bill Smith, this kid in our class. When they see him, they'll see right away that he's not college material."

"But why? What's wrong with Bill Smith?"

"Why, he's—he's a hood. The way he combs his hair, and his clothes are sharp and—oh, you know . . ."

It is of no significance whatsoever and probably due to other reasons that both my young friends were turned down and, curiously enough, that Bill Smith was admitted. Or perhaps like Jove the committee nodded—and, for Bill Smith, in assent.

There is a story that goes the rounds to the effect that one student in making out his application explained that he was not a leader at all but basically a follower, perhaps on the assumption that all other applicants would claim qualities of leadership and the school might want someone for them to practice on. His logic, or his honesty, paid off and he was accepted by the prestige college where he applied. The story is often laughingly quoted by directors of admission as having happened at their own schools when they unbend at an alumni association meeting and lift a corner of the curtain to offer a glimpse into the mystery of their craft.

Whether it is true or apocryphal, it does serve to point up the complete license with which the committee is presumed to operate. Colleges require a fee—usually ten dollars—to accompany the application. Nevertheless, no one thinks he has a right to question a refusal. There is even some vague feeling that "they" are all in cahoots and that to protest a decision at one school would mitigate against a favorable decision in all the others.

It is hard to believe that in a democratic society, on a matter supposedly of such importance, there is so much uncertainty on the one hand and so much willful, indeterminate decision on the other—and so little objection to it. Instead, middle-class families worry and sweat and stew while their young are in high school, especially in the last two years, wondering what "they" will think of this grade, and will "they" understand about this little scrape, and will "they" appreciate the full import of this little triumph or achievement.

We might well ask who "they" are, and on what authority they operate, graciously admitting this one to the good life and peremptorily dismissing that one to outer darkness.

Presumably they perform this function as representatives of the college. But of what segment of the college? Of the faculty? Of the student body? Of the administration? Of the alumni?

I am quite sure that in a large general way the admissions committee represents all of them. Nevertheless, none of these segments of the college has machinery for reviewing the decisions or the overall policies of the admissions committees. If their policies result in insufficient enrollment, or too large an enrollment for the school's facilities, no doubt the administration would have something to say about it. Of equal certainty, if the students chosen were consistently inferior to the point where a sizable number of them were unable to do normal collegiate work, then the grumbling of the faculty would eventually bring about changes. And right now we find student bodies objecting to the choices of the committees on ethnic grounds. As for the alumni, who are also the chief contributors to the endowment fund, there has been evidence through the years that in the recruitment of football players at least they had a large and even a controlling voice.

But with these exceptions, and they are all either extreme or at least highly special cases, it would appear that the admissions committee operates unresponsively and without supervision.

Since the nature of the student body in the long run constitutes the nature of the college, it would appear that the function of the committee is of the highest importance, not merely to young people trying to become part of the college family, but to the college itself. The quota on the basis of race and/or religion is an ugly and undemocratic thing, which is supposed to have disappeared from the college scene; it is only now coming back in reverse, as it were—in the demand that a certain minimum number of Negroes be admitted. But is it certain that a quota system of exclusion of certain segments of our population is not being practiced consciously or unconsciously by admissions committees of various colleges? Absurd? But how can you tell?

One kind of exclusion is certainly being practiced. Almost all but the straight academic type are definitely being excluded by our prestige colleges. In other words, the student body is being recruited in the image of the faculty. The result is a student body that is homogeneous and inbred—and sterile.

The student who has an unusual feeling for nature or an instinctive understanding of people, or who has original ideas that run counter to the academic mind—such a student has little chance of being admitted to the prestige college unless he also has a capacity for getting high marks in all the required subjects. As long as only a reasonable passing grade was required—reasonable in the sense that it indicated that the student could carry on collegiate work—the student of an original turn of mind could get in. But if he has to demonstrate not only capacity but superiority in all subjects, even in those in which he has no great interest, he has little chance of being admitted.

It is frightening to think that some of the great men of our time, men like Winston Churchill, Franklin Roosevelt, or Albert Einstein would not have been admitted to our prestige colleges today.

CHAPTER 9

The Prestige Factor

The thrust toward change rarely occurs along one front. Nor did it in the college and university. There were changes in the thinking of the professoriat about their function. In time this affected the thinking of the administration about the selection of faculty and the selection of their student bodies. Perhaps these changes were preceded by a change in the thinking of society in general and were reactions to it. More likely they interacted with the general thinking of the time.

We might pick as a point of departure the change in the attitude toward research.

To the common man, research meant discovery in the exact sciences—in physics and chemistry and medicine; it gave them wonderful new machines and gadgets and cures for the diseases that had plagued mankind through the centuries. But in

Academe, research meant research in all fields, in literature no less than in physics, in economics no less than in chemistry, in history and music no less than in medicine.

Of course, these last did not lead to great and useful inventions, only perhaps to a paper in a learned journal. And conceivably this was of interest only to a handful of specialists. But the theory was that any research was good. If you nailed down a fact, however minor, even if it had no great significance in and of itself, it might be the point of departure for research that *would* be important.

Once, the view of college administrations was that the function of the professor was to teach; research must not interfere with teaching, but any work in the field that the professor did on his own time was all to the good. If nothing else, it showed an interest in his subject that was above and beyond the demands of his job. His job was to teach; it was what he got paid for. If he chose, on his own time, to engage in research instead of going bowling, it showed that he was truly interested in his subject. And this intensity of interest must of necessity communicate itself to the student. So the teacher who engaged in research was apt to be considered a better teacher, and a long list of publications was of material help in furthering his academic career.

But then the college discovered that there were additional benefits from research. Research conferred prestige, not merely to the researcher but by association to the institution as well. And it was instant prestige.

Formerly, a college had acquired prestige, first, by being old. And then, perhaps, by reason of its illustrious alumni. Here, the older institutions had a distinct advantage; the older they were, the more alumni and the more likelihood of some of them being illustrious. The geographic location helped; schools in the northeastern part of the country were likely to be more prestigious than those in other parts of the country. The size of the endowment contributed, and the physical plant. Other considerations were the prowess of its football team and how often the name of the college appeared in the public press. The latter accounted for the former, of course. A school with a championship football team was frequently mentioned—much more than one that had only a fine faculty and high academic standards.

In short, prestige was a matter of slow growth. But once a member of its faculty did some significant research and made an important discovery, then the result was instant prestige and by association it affected all segments of the school and all who were connected with it. If one faculty member achieved prestige, all faculty members profited. When a professor at the medical school achieved a breakthrough in the cure of a disease, the most junior instructor of English in the liberal arts faculty found his status rising since he was teaching "at the place where that fellow found the cure for German measles." And of course if the English instructor wrote a best-selling novel, then the professor at the medical school profited since he was a colleague of "the guy who wrote that book."

But not only the faculty profited; everyone connected with the university did—students and their parents, alumni, and administration. And this prestige had a hard cash value in addition to its social value. The student of Prestige U. had an easier time getting into a graduate school or getting a job. The instructor interested in switching to another institution for an advanced grade found his connection with Prestige U. extremely helpful. Cow College, with an assistant or associate professorship open, quite naturally gave him preference. As for the professor who had no thought of leaving, his position on the faculty of Prestige U. opened all sorts of lucrative doors—as a consultant to government or big business, as a lecturer, or as a writer of textbooks.

In many ways, the alumnus had the best bargain. With no work on his part, his degree increased in value as the prestige of his alma mater increased. It was a capital gain, like having bought stock in General Motors when it first came on the market, putting it away in a safe deposit box, and then watching it accrue in value. If he were a doctor or a lawyer with his framed degree hanging on his office wall, the effect on his patients or clients left no doubt of the monetary value of the prestige of his college.

And the administration? They gained in every way.

In the matter of staffing their faculties, they were aware that they were leading from strength. They got the pick of the available crop because they were offering something more than just salary—they were offering prestige. And of course, since they were in a strong bargaining position they could choose the more prestigious, or those who were more likely to become prestigious in their own right, and this in turn increased the prestige quotient of the school. Or they could use their bargaining position to offer lower salaries, especially to the lower ranks of teachers, than prevailed elsewhere and still attract the best candidates.

With their alumni, they were in the position of the board of directors of a corporation that showed increasing profits and dividends year after year. In the haul and struggle over direction and policy that is common between administration and alumni in the American college, the administration of Prestige U. was in a far better position than their alter egos at Cow College. And perhaps most of all, prestige was useful in soliciting funds and endowments from alumni, for the alumnus was more willing to contribute to the endowment fund of his college when he was drawing dividends from his academic investment every year.

With respect to students, Prestige U. was not only assured of a steady supply of applicants even during the Depression when many colleges found it hard to fill their classrooms, but, as the number of applicants increased from year to year, they were able to raise their standards accordingly. Some of the more prestigious institutions are able to limit their enrollment to the top 2 percent of secondary school graduates—geniuses all, by the definition of modern psychology. For the faculty, the advantage of having a class made up entirely of quiz kids is obvious; you don't have to teach them at all, you have only to give them assignments. And these your graduate assistant can do just as well if you are busy with some research problem or are on assignment to some government agency.

What a prospect this opened up! Students who had read almost as widely in the field as the professor, who nodded at the most obscure of his references and smiled knowingly at his little scholarly jokes even when they involved outrageous puns in Latin, who asked only the intelligent questions that enabled him to lay open for them the deepest implications of his theories, who could follow with intelligence and understanding the most complex sinuosities of logic in his lectures. Lectures? What need to lecture to a group like this? An assignment—not even that—a mere suggestion that a certain area might repay exploration and they would go to work instantly. Conversations of scintillating wit in the dining halls, flashes of coruscating intelligence in the clubrooms. O brave new world!

Prestige was thus useful in procuring faculty, soliciting endowment, recruiting students, maintaining academic standards, and in resisting the pressure of alumni. It is hardly to be wondered at then, when research produced prestige and prestige conferred all these goodies, that college administrations began to adopt a new attitude toward research. No longer was it regarded as a mere indication of the better teacher because it implied greater interest in his subject, but it now began to be regarded as a good in itself, as the chief characteristic to be sought in an applicant to a position on the faculty. In time, faculty began to be hired primarily to do research and only incidentally to teach; and then it was not long before the teaching function came to be regarded as a means of subsidizing the research and the teaching position a mere sinecure.

Now research takes time and teaching takes time, and there is only so much time. So if the research function was the more important by far, arrangements were made to lighten the teaching load in order to permit more time for research. The fifteen- or sixteen-hour-week work load was reduced to ten or twelve and then for the favored, to six hours, three hours, and even to no hours. At the same time, those members of the faculty who preferred teaching were put on notice that if they expected advancement—and those who were not on tenure, if they wished to keep their jobs—to get busy and do research. Publish or perish!

It was no use complaining that if one spent time on research one would be unable to do an adequate job of teaching. The administration didn't care about teaching. So long as the students didn't object or actually rebel, at least not to the point of getting in the newspapers, the administration was satisfied.

As a result, the view of the nature of the college was shifted. Instead of thinking of the school as intended for the instruction of young people, the idea was developed that it is primarily a guild of scholars in which the students are apprentices and learn by looking over the shoulders of their professors. The orientation of the college shifted from the student to the professor.

CHAPTER 10

What It Costs

The young man who is finishing high school and about to make application for admission to college spends many a long hour poring over a book published by the College Board people and brought up to date every year: it gives brief descriptions of all the colleges in the country with short summaries of their educational philosophy, estimates of the cost of tuition and living expenses, the number of men students and the number of women students, and the ratio of teachers to students. When I was planning on college, there was no such book and none was necessary. I knew that if I passed my College Board exams, I would be admitted to college and that the college I would go to would be one of those within commuting distance of my home in Boston. There were half a dozen or so in the vicinity, although a couple of them were for women, and one was a Catholic school. Tuition was roughly the same at all of them, about three hundred dollars a year.

My parents, though comfortable, were in modest circumstances. I did not get the impression that my going to college imposed any great strain on their finances. If I had gone away to school, it would have been a burden for I would have had to pay for board and lodging and my being away would not have diminished their expenses at all. My room would have been vacant and it would probably have cost my mother as much to cook for two as it did for three.

But when, some twenty-five years later, my daughter was getting ready to go to college, although I was earning a great deal more than my father had when I went, the strain was considerable. I was no longer living within easy commuting distance of a college, but even if I had been, there was no assurance that my daughter would have been accepted there. No one could be sure of getting into any particular college, so you applied to several—anywhere from three for the most optimistic to six or eight for the more pessimistic, and enclosed a ten dollar application fee with each—and hoped that you would be accepted by at least one of them. Going to college, therefore, meant going away from home with the additional expense of boarding and lodging as well as travel between home and school during vacations added to a tuition cost that was already three times what I had paid. So we pored over the summaries in the book, reading the statements of educational philosophy as though they were gospel and discussed the relative merits of size and geographic location. My daughter was quite naturally interested in the ratio of men to women in the student body—an important consideration to a girl. I was a good deal more interested in the student-teacher ratio, which ranged from as many as twenty to one down to as few as four. Imagine it, one teacher for every four pupils. What an educational paradise that conjures up!

I suppose the freshman who has just matriculated at Prestige U. which claims a student-teacher ratio of four to one, who has through the long summer imagined cozy little scenes of himself and three other classmates sitting around a table with a famous professor—sitting there right next to him—or perhaps since there are only four of them, meeting at his house, sitting in comfortable leather armchairs while Mrs. Professor graciously serves coffee, and who then finds that Smith 11, the room where his first class in Economics A meets is an amphitheater of some five hundred seats, all of which are full when he arrives and he has to make do as best he can on the steps in one of the aisles—I suppose that this could be considered his first step in the long educational process, a lesson in reality, the first realization that statistics must be interpreted to be understood.

The college did not lie and the book did not misquote them. The figure of four was arrived at by dividing the total number of students by the total number on the faculty. And there was indeed one faculty member for every four students. But where so many of the faculty teach only a couple of courses, and so many teach only one, and some teach none at all but perhaps see a couple of students once a month who are working on research papers, then some teachers must teach a great many students to make up the difference. And as long as the acoustics are adequate, there is no reason why five hundred students cannot listen to the lecture as well as five.

Or look at it another way: to support the darlings of the faculty, the researchers and discoverers, in the pedagogical idleness which their work demands, means that others must take on their share of the burden as well as their own. What is more, since these research people must be paid, and well paid, and yet carry so small a share of the teaching load, the operating expenses of the school must rise, like a business firm loaded with sons-in-law of the president.

There are other expenses that they incur for the college. There are the huge laboratories and libraries which were part of the inducement to them to come in the first place. And make no mistake, these serve the faculty and not the student body. The million-volume libraries and the multimillion-dollar laboratories are to the undergraduate as an eight-course dinner is to a man on a Sippy diet; it's available, but he can't make use of it. Of course, he can take pride in pointing them out to some country cousin who comes to visit him, but as far as his own needs are concerned, a library of fifty thousand volumes is more than adequate and the apparatus that he will use in his science courses could be housed in his bedroom.

Of course, libraries and laboratories also confer prestige by themselves, as do any large buildings to some degree. But they are expensive—expensive to construct and, even when donated, expensive to maintain. And these expenses, too, are paid for in whole or in part from tuition fees. But since enrollment has not been increased, then tuition fees must be.

Not the least benefit of the prestige factor has been that the demand for admission and the uncertainty of acceptance has made it relatively easy to raise tuition fees. Applicants are so happy at being admitted that they do not cavil at the increased cost. As a result, fees have been increased with considerable regularity in ever-increasing amounts and, curiously enough, with increasing ease. When tuition was five or six hundred dollars, an increase of two hundred dollars would have appeared rapacious, but when tuition stands at two thousand, an increase of two hundred is only 10 percent.

The college tries to make the increase more palatable to the student by representing that his fee covers only a small part of the cost of educating him. They urge that they spend many, many times more on him than he contributes. They arrive at this figure by dividing their total annual expense, including amortization of plant, by the total number of students in residence. I am no economist, but this reasoning is specious. It is like a lion and a mouse sharing a dinner and dividing the cost by two.

And while the college sheds crocodile tears about its need to raise tuition fees to meet ever-increasing costs, it continues to recruit high-scoring students with subsidies and scholarships precisely in the way that has become commonplace in the recruitment of athletes. The reason given is that the college feels it is its duty to ensure the exceptional student an education—

the same pious excuse that was used to justify athletic scholarships in the early days before it became commonplace. The real reason, of course, is that the quiz kid has potential prestige value.

Tuition fees have increased, steadily, constantly, and astronomically in recent years, until now, at prestige colleges in the Northeast, rates are around $2,500 a year. For tuition alone! Add another $2,000 to cover board, lodging, travel to and from school during vacations, books, and student fees, and you have a minimum figure of $4,500 per year to keep a boy at college. And except for the $600 dependency allowance, it is not tax deductible.

Consider an average middle-class family—from which the college community is largely drawn—with two children spaced three years apart. One year both children will be in college at the same time, and if the elder goes on to graduate school—and these days he is likely to—an expenditure of $9,000 will be involved for several years running. Query: How can it be managed when it may represent more than half the total income of the head of the family?

There are a number of solutions, none of them entirely satisfactory. There is, first of all, the possibility of a scholarship, some few of them sufficient to cover the entire cost of college education, including board, lodging, books, even spending money. Obviously, these are few indeed and call for the demonstration of extraordinary talents. For most students the likelihood of achieving such a scholarship is about as great as having it left under the pillow by the Tooth Fairy. Lesser sums are available, usually keyed to need as determined by a statement of his net worth made by the parent. This is helpful, but demeaning to a man who has always prided himself on paying his own way.

Another objection to the scholarship system is that some students feel that since they are being sustained in part by the benevolence of the school, they are no longer free agents. Some colleges go to great lengths to separate the scholarship committee from administrative pressure and influence in order to eliminate or at least to minimize this reaction on the part of the scholarship recipient. Nevertheless, the student is apt to have an instinctive feeling for the realities of the situation and will usually take care to keep his grades up and to conform.

The federal government also grants loans through the colleges, and these do not have to be repaid until some time after graduation. There is a general feeling that even when it is time to begin paying off the loan, there is no great pressure if one cannot make the payments. One is not subjected to the harassment that one would suffer for failure to pay one's income tax, for example. Furthermore, it feels different to receive aid from the government from the way it does to take a handout from the college. In the latter case, some work might be involved like waiting on table in the student cafeteria, but the government loan is to that extent without strings. And what is more, it is sanctioned by custom—feeding at the public trough is an old American tradition. Perhaps for all these reasons, the government loan is the best form of aid. Unfortunately, the maximum covers only a small portion of the total expense of going to one of the private prestige colleges.

The fine old custom of working one's way through college is nowadays discouraged. It is questionable whether it ever was a good idea. College years are the time for the development of new ideas and this calls for leisure. The poor student who raced through the dormitory collecting students' laundry and then dashed to the student cafeteria to wash dishes and wait on table, finishing just in time to get to class if he hurried, may have managed to get passing grades in all his courses, perhaps even honor grades, but frequently that was all he got—just grades, no education.

But, of course, the college authorities do not discourage the student's parents from working. If the head of the family is not already moonlighting, and his wife working, to pay for color television, two cars, and a house on a nice street, then of course he can and she can in order to put their pride and joy through a fine college. There probably will be no embarrassment since their son, although aware of what they are doing, will probably have the good taste not to mention it.

And finally, the young man can go to a less expensive school, a state college, perhaps, where the tuition is anywhere from $100 to $500 or $600 instead of $2,000 or more. In many families this is the poorest solution. It is not merely that the father has a chauvinistic affection for his alma mater and has been looking forward to the day when his son will matriculate there, he is also imbued with the idea couched in the cliché that you get what you pay for. If the tuition at Prestige U. is $2,400 per year and tuition at State U. is only $200 per year, then obviously instruction at Prestige is a dozen times better than that at State U. The parent regards the college as a kind of knowledge emporium where you buy education in much the same way that you buy food in a food store and clothing in a clothing store. To buy knowledge at the state university is like buying clothing in the bargain basement; it may be good value for the money, but the fit is uncertain, the tailoring poor, the material sleazy.

If his son should nevertheless go to State, the parent, for his own peace of mind, and to quiet his feeling of guilt, will reflect that the $200 tuition fee is only a small part of the cost and that the State bears the burden of the rest. But the uncomfortable feeling will persist that he has failed to provide adequately for his son's future, and that he is doing less for him than *his* father did for him.

CHAPTER 11

Effects on the Secondary School

The prestige colleges number three or ten or twenty-five, in any case a handful, depending on your point of view. If you are from the Northeast and particularly if you or some member of your family is a graduate of Harvard, say, you may allow the title to Yale and Princeton and then perhaps if pressed, grudgingly admit a couple of women's colleges like Radcliffe, Wellesley and Bryn Mawr. If you are from other sections of the country, you will no doubt think of many more, but in any case it will be a mere handful in comparison with the total number of colleges in the country.

What then is so important about the prestige college? How much weight does its trickle of graduates carry against the veritable tide that flows from the rest?

The fact is, of course, that the prestige colleges, insignificant though their numbers are whether in terms of students or faculty, are the leaders that set the pace in the academic world. The direction taken by the prestige college is the direction that will be taken after a while by all the others.

Even the state colleges, in varying degrees controlled by and responsive to the state legislatures and hence to the electorate, their admissions policies regulated by state law, follow the lead of the prestige colleges in the matter of admissions, just as they do in the matter of organization, curriculum, and standards. With impunity, the state college does this with respect to applicants from out of state; indeed, there is a natural tendency to raise standards for out-of-towners since the more difficult it is to get in, the better the school is presumed to be.

But even for residents of the state, the state college can follow the lead of the prestige colleges and bypass the clear intent of the regulation by various devices. For one thing, the state college, while constantly expanding its facilities to meet the demand, is never in any one year big enough to take all residents of the state who are qualified and who request admission. So they are in the position of having to make a selection and they usually do it along prestige college lines—on a competitive basis.

More recently, they have succeeded in setting up a hierarchy of institutions of higher education. There is at the top, the state university which in addition to the liberal arts college has graduate schools and is authorized to grant graduate degrees. And even here, if there are separate branches in various parts of the state, there may be a difference in the admissions standards between one branch and another.

Then there are the four-year state colleges, formerly teachers' colleges, which usually are not empowered to grant graduate degrees, at least not above the Master's, and this usually a Master of Education degree. Finally, there are a number of two-year community or junior colleges usually located in or near the large centers of population. Applicants to the university whose grades are not high enough are shunted off to seek admission at the four-year college and they in turn encourage the lower ranking of their applicants to apply for admission to the junior colleges with the promise that if they do well, they can, on graduation, transfer into the junior year of a four-year college.

But the influence of the prestige college is not only felt in the general world of higher education, but also in the lower schools—the high school and the junior high school. The immediate effect in the high school is naturally on the college preparatory course. What the college demands, the high school will supply. As the college developed the competitive system of admissions, the high schools developed the track system, a kind of screening device whereby the quicker students are segregated from the rest so that they can be given more work and thus get special preparation for competing with pupils from other schools for admission to the better colleges.

Again it seems like a reasonable arrangement: divide the total into groups according to their seeming capacities and then teach each group separately. Then the slow ones will not hold back the quick ones and will not themselves be hurried along beyond their capacity. This kind of separation and segregation is normal in sports contests, for example, such as boxing and wrestling, where small men compete against small men and large men against large.

But of course the capacity of a body—its size, its weight, its strength—can be measured with great exactness. There is a positive and easily demonstrated correlation between the force of a blow and the mass behind it. A heavyweight strikes a much harder blow than a featherweight, not to mention that the size of his body permits him to take a punch with less damage.

In the matter of learning, however, we are dealing with the mind, and devices for measuring it, primarily the intelligence test, are woefully inadequate. They measure only a few out of a myriad of mental traits, and since the test carries a time limit, what is being tested is primarily speed of reaction. But it has never been demonstrated that speed of mental reaction correlates positively with total mental capacity.

Anyone who has ever played chess beyond the home amusement level is aware that there are quick movers and slow movers, and that the former are not better than the latter. The quick mover seems to see the position on the board instantly, almost intuitively. As he studies the board, the position does not become clearer. On the contrary, the first effect is a confusion of the mind in which the understanding of the situation on the board is less clear than it was just before, when he understood it intuitively. True, if he perseveres, the confusion is gradually dispelled and he will see the position with greater clarity than he did at first. The slow mover, on the other hand, begins with a confused picture which clarifies steadily as he studies the position.

Under ordinary conditions of play, the slow mover wins at least as often as does the quick mover when they play against each other. In so-called rapid-transit chess, where only a few seconds are permitted for each move, the quick mover of course does better. But under normal conditions of play, the quick mover is frequently a victim of his own quickness. He finds it harder to concentrate in a difficult situation, tends to become impatient, and finally makes the move that first occurred to him.

As a parent and a teacher, I have observed similar differences in the responses of young people to the learning process. So, to divide pupils by intelligence test scores is to divide on the basis of a single measuring device, one that primarily tests speed of mental reaction. This is like dividing all athletes on the basis of their speed in the hundred-yard dash with no consideration of such other faculties as the ability to run a long distance or to jump or to strike a ball or to lift a weight.

Other effects of the track system must be considered. There is the effect on the classroom situation. The segregation of the quick minds produces an unrealistic situation in the classroom. In an unsegregated class the quick-witted students serve as pacemakers and spurs to their slower classmates who respond to the challenge. Nor does the quick-witted student lose by the situation. There is a kind of mental exhilaration in the interaction between his mind and the rest of the class that in turn spurs him on to greater endeavor.

The usual criticism of the nontrack system is that the bright pupil, held back by the dullness of his classmates, loses interest. The implication is that we should shed crocodile tears over the loss to society of all the bright youngsters who lost interest in study and were stultified by the mediocrity of their classmates before the introduction of the track system. It futher suggests that the learning process is carried on solely in the classroom. Actually, the students who found classroom work insufficiently challenging for their eager minds undertook work on their own. The classroom assignment of a few scenes from a Shakespearean play might be insufficient to maintain the interest of the bright student, but there was nothing to prevent him from reading the play in its entirety and then going on to read others. Indeed, it is the common experience in families for a bright child to spend much of his spare time in reading while his less studious brothers and sisters play or watch television.

Another aspect of the track system is that the student soon finds that it is a railroad track; he is on rails and cannot get off. Formerly, the student started each year with a clean slate. If he had done poorly in one grade, he had a chance to show his mettle the following year in the next grade. His record the previous year, unless he had actually failed, did not follow him or weigh him down like an incubus the next year. But under the track system, although he can fall from grace and be dropped from a higher track to a lower, he cannot climb from a lower to a higher because he will not have had the additional work that is taken in the higher track. The slow starters, those whose minds develop a little later than the average, are particularly hurt by the system.

I understand that it is commonplace nowadays for private kindergartens to give intelligence or aptitude exams to all applicants for admission. One parent who had just been through this harrowing and traumatic experience reported that after the grading he was informed that his child, although of college material, would probably not make a prestige school. Would even God venture such a prediction?

My town prides itself on its progressive school system, which means that they are readily persuaded to try almost any new educational device or gimmick that comes along. Naturally, they have a track system and it starts with the primary grades. But until the seventh grade, the subjects and curriculum remain pretty much the same. Then, however, the system becomes vicious and the real separation of the sheep from the goats takes place. One group is segregated on the basis of a combination of marks, I.Q.'s, and teachers' opinions. These, the cream of the student body, not only have different subjects and proceed at a more rapid pace, they even have a different set of teachers. These are the ones that are being groomed for the prestige colleges.

There is nothing secret about it. It is not just another section of the grade. The parents of the children are notified and the children themselves know that they are a special group. They are the new Elect, but they are on rails and they are off and running.

For a few days the children are indignant that their best friends of the previous grade have not also been chosen; and their parents preen themselves on their good fortune and hypocritically assure the parents of those who were less fortunate that it doesn't really mean anything and that their children have just as much of a chance of getting into a good college as their own. But then they buckle down to work, both parents and children. They've got to produce if they want to stay in the section. They're not home by a long way. All that has happened is that the child has managed to be among the qualifiers in the first trial heat.

Even if the parent is unable to give active participatory help on home lessons, he is expected at least to ride herd on his offspring, check to see that he has done his homework every night and is not goofing off. Father and son pore over the textbook, arguing about what a question really calls for—because naturally any real red-blooded American father wants to help his own son—and besides it makes for a closer relationship: pals. And the son, too, has been conditioned to believe that he likes it, just like Little League with his father right there in the stands shouting encouragement to him when he is up at bat, or sorrowfully criticizing—"You weren't concentrating, son. You took your eye off the ball and kind of daydreamed there for a moment" —when he struck out.

I was present once at a meeting of the principal with the parents of this group, when one father rose to complain about a home lesson that the French teacher had assigned. She had asked her pupils to run through whatever magazines there were around the house and to list any French words they came across. "My boy and I spent two and a half hours looking through my magazines. I'll admit they're all on electronic engineering, but all we could come up with was two words. Now what kind of home lesson is that? Why couldn't she have given him a list of words to memorize? How are we going to beat the Russians that way?"

Comes report card time and young Claude, trepidant, presents his record of achievement to his father for signature. A nod of approval at the B minus in history that had been brought up from a C plus, and then a frown as he sees that there has been no change in the mark of C in mathematics.

"What did Billy get in math?"

A shrug of the shoulders. "I don't know."

"Well, I know because his father was telling me on the train coming in this morning. He got a B. That's what he got. When did you get this report card?

"Today."

"Then how come Dick Smith knew what Billy was getting this morning?"

"She read the marks out yesterday."

"And you didn't think to mention what your mark was. Right? And I don't wonder. If I got a C in math, I'd be ashamed too." And he thinks how he will feel tomorrow when Smith asks him what Claude got in math and he has to say he got a C.

A shrug.

"What chance do you think you have of getting into a good

college with marks like this? It's only four years away, you know."

Four years, four centuries, four eternities to Claude. Why, almost anything could happen in four years. The atom bomb might fall. His father might die and he'd be able to leave school and go to work. He himself might be lucky and die. But Claude doesn't say any of this, because even if he's not so hot in math, he's A plus in knowing what the old man will stand for and what will send him up like a rocket. So he whines, "Well *his* father helps him."

"Don't I help you? You telling me that Smith's math is better than mine?"

"No, but he doesn't just explain it. They go over every problem together and he checks Billy's answers."

"Well, maybe that's what we'd better do from now on. Now you go right up to your room and work on your math, and then you come down and we'll go over it."

Exit Claude, and his mother enters the list. "Why are you always picking on him? That was a pretty good report card. He didn't fail anything."

"Because pretty good is not good enough. These days you've got to be damn good or you end up in some little jerkwater college that nobody ever heard of and what chance have you got to get a decent job with a degree from a place like that? I'm doing it for him, aren't I? Isn't that why we moved here from the city, so he could go to a good school?"

CHAPTER 12

Effects on the Core City

There were any number of reasons for the abandonment of the core city and the trek to the suburbs after World War II; a better school system was one of them. Not only did the suburbs offer a better school for those planning to go on to college, but there was also the feeling that the very fact that you came from a good suburb gave you a better chance of acceptance by a good college.

It was after you came to the suburbs that you began to see why the school system was better. The town was small. If it was in New England, it might even have a town meeting form of government. Every year the various departments of the town—the police, the firemen, the school department—had to come before the town meeting for the approval of their budgets for the following year. And almost every year, they wanted something: a raise in pay, additions to the force, new buildings, new equipment. So they tended to be pleasant and responsive to the taxpayer who was also the voter.

If you had some criticism of the school system, you were heard because your vote was important. The town was small, you knew people and you could talk to them and they were all taxpayers and voters. The Parent-Teacher Association was not just a monthly meeting where the principal said a few words of greeting and then let you wander about the classrooms to see the exhibits on the walls. It was really an association of teachers and parents where you spoke your piece and where, by God, the teachers listened.

And because in most suburbs you had to buy a house instead of renting, and it was fairly expensive, the chances were that your fellow townsmen, at least all the new ones, were fairly well fixed and planned to send their children to college, to good colleges. So the schools were responsive to their demands and to their needs. Some parents indeed were still not satisfied and sent their children to private schools, but the great majority worked to improve the public schools as college preparatory systems.

It snowballed. The better the suburban schools became, the more people were attracted to the suburbs, and the fewer people were left in the core city who were interested in college for their children. And this, in turn, meant that there were fewer people left in the core city who were interested in the school system, and this attitude in turn influenced the behavior of their children. To them, the school was simply a place they had to go until they finished. They weren't going on. So it wasn't important how good or how bad they were, because they were just there marking time until they got that little old diploma. And if it wasn't important to them or to their parents, then it wasn't important to the school committee or the city administration. It was certainly not important to the people who lived in the suburbs and commuted to the core city to work. In a negative way, it *was* important to the large taxpayers, the owners of large taxable properties who also lived in the suburbs: they wanted as little as possible spent on the schools because every extra dollar spent increased the tax rate.

As far as teachers were concerned, the old ones who had tenure and had got used to it over the years stayed on. But the younger ones, the new teachers, the idealistic ones, were naturally drawn to the suburban school systems where the pupils were eager and the pay frequently better.

So the core city continued to decay, the schools getting poorer and poorer, the buildings shabbier and more decrepit, the equipment and the books and the curriculum more and more out of date. And here too, there is a snowball effect, because while a new building commands a certain respect, an old decaying structure seems to invite abuse and vandalism. Several cracked windows suggest, seem to call for, the hurled stone. Badly marked desks invite the jackknife. Graffiti begets graffiti. Until suddenly, something happens to make the citizens aware that they have permitted their school system to deteriorate to the point where they are below par—a feature story in the local newspaper, perhaps, complete with pictures of the toilets, of the peeling paint in the classrooms, of the single low-watt bulb that lights a stairway. Or it may be the committee of a national educational association making a survey of school systems in large cities; or an investigating group sponsored by the Chamber of Commerce or Rotary that first makes the announcement. There is a hue and cry. Letters are written to the newspapers. Demands are made on the school committee.

Then comes the cream of the jest: the local prestige college, whose competitive admissions policies have had so much to do with starting the ball rolling downhill, volunteers or is requested by the city government to send in a task force of professors to evaluate the situation and make recommendations as to what should be done.

CHAPTER 13

Effect on the College

When I was a small boy, I played marbles and tops, and baseball and football after a fashion. We played because we wanted to, not because we were urged or even encouraged by our parents. Our parents didn't send us out to play; they merely sent us out—to get us out from underfoot. They didn't usually buy our equipment for us either. We bought our marbles and tops with the pennies we were given for candy. Bigger stuff like a baseball glove or a pair of skates or a sled, we might be given as birthday or Christmas gifts—after considerable hinting on our parts; parents were inclined to think of things like a checker game or dominoes or Parcheesi or even a book as more suitable. Certainly, it never occurred to them to buy us these things because they were necessary to our development.

Marbles and tops being games that two or three could play, we usually played with youngsters of our own age. But baseball and football were team games and there were never enough youngsters in an age group in the neighborhood to make up two teams, so everyone from eight to fifteen was apt to take part. In baseball the younger boy played in the outfield where he was useful in retrieving balls. When it got to be his turn at bat, the pitcher would throw him an easy ball so he could hit it or at least strike at it. Otherwise, he might stand there at the plate refusing pitch after pitch and hold up the game. There were no called strikes since there was no umpire to call them. The batter remained at the plate until he had struck the ball or swung at it three times.

In football, the younger ones were drafted into the line positions, while the older ones ran the ball or kicked it or threw it. There were no coaches, no managers, no cheering section; any youngster who came along was usually included in the game. We did not keep score, and the game ended when it got dark, or when we were called in to supper.

Of course, none of this is possible today. Parents see to it that their children play because it's good for them, good for their bodies and their coordination and their group integration, and to give harmless release to their antisocial drives and all kinds of things that the social scientists have been able to name. Children play in a playground and there's a supervisor, probably with a degree in physical education, who organizes the play with blasts on a little whistle suspended from his neck by a string. He gives instruction in the approved techniques for knuckling a marble. And if he sees a youngster who shows a special aptitude for it, he grooms him for the state championships.

Children's baseball is played by uniformed teams with the best of equipment on a regulation diamond. Each team in the league has a coach and maybe an assistant coach—and they really coach. When the teams play, there is an umpire in a blue serge suit with a mask and a chest protector and a little whisk broom to brush off home plate. And the parents are in this regular grandstand to cheer on their kids.

The same thing with football. And to make sure that the kids realize the importance of it all, they make a regular ceremony of the opening day of the season. I happened to be taking a walk in the early fall and I noticed that groups of people, in twos and threes, were standing around on the sidewalk expectantly. People don't usually stand around on the sidewalk in my town, at least not in my part of it. So I too stopped, and presently I heard the sound of martial music as if a parade was approaching. And by God it was a parade and that's what they were waiting for. First came the high school band in uniform. Then came a couple of fire trucks. Then the selectmen marching all abreast. And then another band—this one a bagpipe band in kilts, a spin-off of our local hand-pump brigade. And then came a horde of youngsters, helmeted and shoulder-padded and thigh-padded and cleated like midgets from Mars. Like other bystanders, I followed them to the playground where the flag was raised and the bands in unison played "God Bless America." And then the half dozen teams sorted themselves out and were put through some snappy last-minute signal drill before taking the field.

The other day, after a snowfall, I saw some children coasting down a short hill. They were all ages—anywhere from five to twelve or thirteen. Some had sleds and some had large aluminum saucers. There were even a couple who had a large cardboard packing case which they had flattened out and which seemed just as effective for sliding down the short hill. They seemed to be having a lot of fun. I found myself wondering how long it would be before their elders organized it and arranged for regular competitions.

But it's not only the children; it's the adults, too. A friend of mine who has a fine baritone voice got connected with a barbershop quartet. For a while he was full of the pleasures of four-part *a cappella* singing. Then he told me he was going down to Worcester the following night to a competition of barbershop quartets. It seems there's a nationwide organization and they compete regularly. And there's a whole big system of accredited judges with all kinds of rules and points and you can advance in the organization as a judge just as you can as a member of a quartet. And the same thing is true of amateur theatricals and square dancing. And of course everybody knows about bridge.

All this competition, this insane desire not to enjoy something but to prove oneself better at it than the rest—where does it end? Not in college certainly, most certainly not in the prestige college. One would like to think that Claude, having fought the good fight, is now prepared to reap the reward of his efforts and enjoy his four years wandering through the academic grove. Not so. It is in college, especially in the prestige college, that the pace really picks up.

For one thing, the A.B. degree is no longer regarded as terminal. From time immemorial, commencement day orators made a point of explaining that graduation was called commencement because it signified that the student's education was just beginning. What he meant, of course, was that the young man was now going out into the world and was about to begin his education in reality. He was speaking figuratively. Now, however, commencement is really only a beginning; it marks the beginning of graduate study. Remember that the student body at Prestige U. is handpicked. They were selected not merely on the basis of their grades in high school and their College Board exam scores, but also on their orientation and motivation, on their plans and aspirations for the future. So it is not surprising that between 70 and 90 percent of the graduates of Prestige U. go on to graduate study.

But admission to the graduate school, both the professional schools and the graduate schools of arts and sciences, is apt to be even more difficult than admission to the liberal arts college. So the college student must prove in his four years his right to a place in the graduate school. He must get top grades, because he is in competition with his classmates who also want to get into a graduate school; only now he is competing in a bigger league. Then again, a much larger share of the students are on scholarships and fellowships, or are competing for them.

The most obvious result has been a phenomenal rise in the incidence of cheating. It has been estimated that in some colleges as many as 50 percent of the students cheat in their examinations.

What is particularly alarming is that most of the cheating is now done by the good students trying for a high grade rather than the poor students who used to do it to avoid flunking out. In this same connection college librarians report that students steal books from the library that are necessary or useful in preparing for a particular exam, not so that they can study them at their leisure in the dormitory, but to prevent their competing classmates from using them.

One kind of cheating has become so common that it goes unremarked. Indeed, it is no longer regarded as cheating. This is the use of the printed outline and summary of required reading material. At one time they were forbidden and students purchased them secretly. Now, they are on sale in all college bookstores and many of them are written by professors of well-considered college faculties.

In an English literature course, for example, one can get summaries of all the reading, including the usual correct critical opinions, an outline of the major developments of the period covered, along with the catch phrases that characterize them. It gives the student enough to pass the examination in the course and even to get an honor mark, without having read *any* of the original work, and perhaps without having attended a lecture. Since the information in the outline is in capsule form, it is readily assimilable, and the student using it may do better on the examination than the student who has done all the required reading and attended all the lectures. He is certain to do better if the latter is so foolhardy as to do his own thinking and offer his own critical opinions; the ones in the outline are the "correct" ones. The instructor, in reading the blue books can usually tell which of his students have used the outlines, but there is nothing he can do about it, nothing he would want to do about it since the questions have been answered and the answers are correct.

Since the purpose of the examination is to test whether the student has done the reading and understood it and followed and assimilated the lectures, this use of the outline is obviously cheating. And that the student is cheating himself makes it no less reprehensible.

And yet a case could be made out to justify this short cut to knowledge. As the caliber of the students improved, the instructor felt that he could safely demand more of them—not more thought, not even work at a higher level, merely a greater volume of work, more in the pail. Each instructor seemed bent on upgrading his courses by making them harder, until the total volume of work for the student in all his courses was so great as to leave him no time for himself, no time for contemplation, no time for reading for pleasure. The professorial thumb was always there, goosing him to do more text reading, to write reports, to do more research. So the printed outline could be considered the student's defensive weapon in his constant duel with the instructor.

It may be simply nostalgia on my part, but I remember college as an extremely pleasant place and the four years I spent as an undergraduate as one of the high points of my life. Thinking back, it seems to me that my classmates felt much the same way. The work was not hard and we had plenty of free time to sit for hours in restaurants over coffee and cigarettes, talking and arguing. We had time to think and to incorporate what we learned in the classroom with our own experience. It is only my opinion, based on casual observation, but I have the feeling that modern college students do not enjoy college. For one thing, there is a lot of shifting from one college to another these days. If students really liked college, I don't think they would transfer so readily. They may like the freedom from parental control that it gives them; they may enjoy whatever prestige it confers on them; they may take pleasure in the companionship of people of their own age and background that it affords; but I don't feel that the modern student enjoys college as an intellectual experience. They haven't the time. They are too harried and harassed.

We didn't have a resident staff of counselors and psychiatrists in the colleges in the old days. I am not suggesting that it is a superfluous, modern frill; quite the contrary, I think we should have more. The suicide rate among college students is one and a half times what it is among young people of the same age group who are not in college.

CHAPTER 14

How Good Are Marks?

Our educational system is a competition in which the rewards go to those with the highest marks. But what, precisely, are high marks, and how are they obtained?

Is there a positive correlation between the high mark and high intelligence—even equating intelligence to the extremely limited mental characteristics that are the medium of exchange in our present school system? That is, we do not teach grace and rhythm and virtue and fellowship and sensitivity and orderliness and the thousand and one other admirable attributes of the human animal in our schools and colleges, and we do not give marks in them. We *do* teach history and math and physics, and it is the marks that are given in these that count. Well, is there even a correlation between high understanding in these few subjects and the high marks that are given to the favored few?

In a very general way and with a reasonable regard for exceptions, of course there is. The lad in high school who consistently gets A's in math probably has a better grasp of the subject than the boy who with equal consistency gets C's. Whether he understands the subject any better than the boy who regularly gets B pluses is something else again. But the competition at each level is keen and what is required for admission to the prestige colleges is not merely a special aptitude in math or history or English, but high marks in all subjects. Similarly, Dean's List in college means honor grades in all courses. And here, an uncomfortable thought obtrudes. It is normal to be interested in one subject rather than in another. This usually means that the subject that one likes comes easier and a high mark is easier to attain in it than in subjects that one does not like. And this in turn suggests that in order to get high marks in all subjects, the competitive student must spend more time on those he does not care about than he does on those he likes and finds interesting. The usual procedure for the student on the make, therefore, is to do just enough work in the course he's truly interested in to get the necessary A, and then spend the rest of his time working on the courses he does not care for in order to get A's in them as well. And this gives rise to the suspicion that the Dean's List student is not so much interested in learning and study as he is in getting good marks.

This knack or capacity for getting good marks is the one characteristic that all high-ranking students have in common. And this is the only common characteristic we can say with certainty that they have. Some work hard for their grades and some seemingly do not. Some are seemingly engrossed exclusively in their studies, while others may have many outside interests. Some are liked by their classmates and some are disliked. Some are noisy and outgoing, others are quiet and withdrawn. They show as many differences in personality and character as they do in physical appearance. Curiously enough, they do not even correlate to high I.Q.'s, although it would not be surprising if they did, since this is also a mark and their particular knack could manifest itself on the intelligence test as well. Certainly, the high-ranking student who shows no common sense is not an uncommon phenomenon.

There is nothing mysterious in this knack for getting high marks; after all, marks are given on the basis of the work done in the class, on tests, quizzes, and examinations. The questions on examinations as well as the questions asked by the teacher in class all have an expected reply. When the teacher asks a question, whether orally in class or on a written examination, he has the answer in mind. The student who gives him the answer he has in mind has answered the question correctly, and if it is not the answer he has in mind, the teacher's first reaction is that it is wrong. Even if it is a plausible answer, a reasonable and logical answer, if not wrong in the teacher's mind, it is certainly not as good as the one he wanted and expected. That is only human nature, and the teacher is all too human. So the student who senses what the teacher wants to hear, and gives it to him, even if he doesn't agree with it, is the student who will get the good mark. The special knack that he has, then, is first an idea of what the teacher wants to hear by way of an answer, in and of itself not too difficult, and second, a willingness to give it to him, even if it is contrary to his own thinking.

In many cases, it is simply a matter of giving back to the teacher the answer he had given earlier in his original instruction. So this could be either an indication that the student was listening attentively, or it might indicate that he doesn't bother to think through the subject matter of the course on his own but is content to accept without question what the teacher tells him.

The student who gives the teacher back what he wants to hear is the one who is likely to get the highest grades. In most cases, he pursues this course because he knows no other. He has never learned to think for himself and knows of no other way of arriving at knowledge than to hear it from someone else, usually the teacher. He need not have a good mind, only a good memory.

On his part, the teacher believes he is completely objective in his marking. He regards the test or the examination as a means of determining how much the student has learned but he thinks of learning very largely in terms of factual information which he received from *his* teacher and which he is now passing on to his students. And theories which he got from his professor or from a textbook have for him the status of proved fact. It is normal for him to assume that the student who gives him back what he has given out, the student who is in agreement with him, is the brightest student. And that the student who gives him some other answer has not studied his lesson and is trying to bluff.

A young colleague, a new instructor giving a course in Freshman English, asked me to look through a set of themes that he had just graded, his first, to see if I concurred in his marking. The class had been reading an essay on ESP and they had been asked to write of some ESP experience that had happened to them or they had heard about. The marks ran largely to C with a light sprinkling of B's. The themes were what might have been expected, highly fanciful accounts of experiences that the students had made up on the spur of the moment; they were written in class. One paper, however, had the ring of truth and it had received the mark of D. I could see why. The entire first page was one long sentence. Even then, the grade seemed unreasonably low, under the circumstances. The young instructor, however, had no doubts. "I considered giving him a flunk mark, F. After all I've said about sentence structure . . ."

"It's this first page, isn't it?" I said. "Let me read it to you." I read it through. "What do you think?"

"Well, if he'd written it like that . . ."

"But he did write it like that," I pointed out. "They are perfectly formed sentences, except that instead of ending each one with a period and starting the next with a capital, he strung them all together with 'ands.' "

My young colleague shook his head slowly in obdurate denial. He couldn't see it. To him a sentence was a sentence was a sentence. It was a matter of punctuation, not a matter of logical arrangement of thought.

Some bright students do indeed have independent ideas but if they are interested in high marks they keep them to themselves and find it politic to agree with the instructor. This type of student is no better off than the other. He will find it politic to pursue the same method all through life. He finds that the method that works in the grade schools works just as well in high school, and in college, and in graduate school, and with his supervisor or department head when he finally gets out of school. In effect, his schooling has stultified him. The method is built into the system; it requires either a teacher of great humility or of extraordinary largeness of mind to tolerate contradiction from his students, and minds of this quality are rare in the teaching fraternity because, to be blunt, the average schoolteacher is second rate.

Among the learned professions, pedagogy stands at the bottom. It is normally the second-rate student who goes into secondary-school teaching. Teachers' colleges and schools of education stand far below other schools of comparable level. The undergraduate teachers' college attracts a poorer student and a less distinguished faculty than does the college of liberal arts. Similarly, the graduate school of education is inferior to the other graduate schools of the university. Graduate degrees in the field of education, both the master's and the doctorate, are universally regarded as being on a lower level than the degrees from liberal arts colleges. There are sectional differences to be sure and these observations are perhaps more true of the Northeast than of other sections of the country, but the fact remains that a student going from a liberal arts college to a graduate school of education doesn't brag about it.

Nor does the milieu of the secondary school do much to expand or improve the mind of the teacher. For the greater part of the day, he is involved with the young and the immature. In his professional work, he meets nonteaching adults only at parent-teacher meetings or on rare occasions when he has an irate parent to contend with. Usually he doesn't mind his isolation from adult society. In his classroom he is king. When he frowns, the class grows quiet; when he unbends to make a small joke, it is greeted with paroxysms of sycophantic laughter, which convinces him that he is a wit and in general quite a fellow.

Two reasons the profession attracts the second rate are its low pay and low social status. There is perhaps a subconscious wisdom in the mass of people, and when they assign a low social status to the teacher it may be not without reason. Certainly, it is a fair assumption that anyone who enters a line of work that will guarantee him a low standard of living does so because he is afraid to compete at a higher level. There is also the suspicion that one who chooses to deal largely with children may be doing so out of fear of facing the adult world.

The argument that teachers may choose the profession in spite of the low pay because it offers them more leisure than would another profession or any other job is largely illusory. The teacher is the first to admit, nay to insist as though there were a special virtue in it, that when his day at the school ends, his work at home begins: he has papers to mark, lesson plans to prepare, and afternoon and evening classes to attend. For many, the summer vacation is not a time of leisure, but rather an opportunity either to attend summer sessions or to take another job to piece out a low salary. In many school systems, the teacher *must* take courses and earn extra credits in order to insure receiving his annual increment. One might raise the obvious question: If the teacher is a professional scholar, why should he have to take courses at all? Should he not be able to prepare a reading list on his own in any subject in which he feels deficient?

I have been discussing the primary and secondary school teacher, those whose judgments and decisions constitute the first and hence perhaps the most important checkpoints in the careers of the children of the country. The situation in the colleges is somewhat more complex. Formerly, college instructors and professors were not too much different from their secondary school colleagues. The fact that they found themselves teaching in college rather than in high school was apt to be quite accidental. An M.A. was usually all that was required, and in the more advanced large city school systems the same degree was required for teaching in the high school. Salaries were either comparable, or, as often as not, the advantage was with the high school. But there was always a small group of true scholars who chose college teaching because although it might pay less, it did offer more free time and more opportunity for further study and research. And the research they did was *real* research, investigation in something that interested them rather than something that was merely publishable.

Nowadays the situation is somewhat different. A sizable percentage of college teachers are still no different in character or ability from secondary school teachers; indeed, many of them taught in secondary schools before taking the college jobs. And there are even a few who leave college teaching to go into high school teaching because it may pay better. The research segment, however, has been drawn off from teaching since it was found that their research confers status and prestige on the college.

In recent years, largely for this very reason, college teaching positions have become much more desirable, and the type of student who formerly would have gone into one of the more lucrative professions is crowding into college teaching. The pay is now better, the hours are much shorter, and the opportunities for additional income from industry and government are good.

Unfortunately, very little of this improvement of the caliber of the faculty redounds to the benefit of the student. The more scholarly the professor, the less teaching he will do; and if he becomes outstanding, he is likely to be engaged in various enterprises, industrial and governmental, that will take up his full time and keep him away from college altogether. His name will continue in the catalog, and he will be the titular teacher of one or more courses, but he will not even be available for consultation, let alone for lectures, since he will be in Washington, or New York, or Paris, or London.

CHAPTER 15

The Scholar

But what of the scholar? True, his actual time in the classroom may be short, but does not the student derive some benefit from him? Does he not absorb some of his mana by osmosis? Is his job at the college a pure sinecure that profits the student who helps pay his salary little or nothing?

There used to be a generally accepted idea, hopelessly old-fashioned now, that the function of the scholar, researcher, scientist, intellectual, in our society was to uphold objective truth in a self-serving, opinionated, partisan, chauvinistic world. Originally, this had been the function of the clergy, whose loyalty to God transcended the smaller loyalties to family, party, or country. After World War I, however, a certain disenchantment with the clergy set in. They had not stood above the battle. All through the war, while the clergy of the Allied Powers prayed to

God for victory and confusion to our enemies, the clergy of the Central Powers were begging the same Deity for the same thaumaturgical favors and in the same liturgical and ecclesiastical forms. It was disillusioning and may have had something to do with the cynicism and agnosticism that characterized the decade that followed.

But the scholar-scientist was pledged to truth, and his devotion did not have to be taken on faith; the results were there for all to see in the form of radios, automobiles, and cures of ancient diseases. Science and scholarship—these were not mere tribal rites, narrow and parochial. They were universal goods that transcended national boundaries. True, a barbarous and jingoistic government could burn books and halt scholarship, but that only proved its essential barbarity. The scientist in the obscurity of his laboratory and the scholar in his study worked only to combat ignorance and to advance the cause of truth. And the university was his natural habitat, an ivory tower that shut out the partisan clamor of the everyday world. He asked only the peace and quiet of the academic grove that permitted him to carry on his studies, and his reward was the respect and approval of his colleagues and the satisfaction of knowing that he had made a contribution to the sum total of man's knowledge.

But with the discovery that research could generate prestige and that prestige could produce all kinds of benefits for the college, the scholar was forced back into the world. Government and big business decided that they could make advantageous use of his special abilities. And the beauty of the arrangement was that he could do both: work for industry and/or the government and retain his position on the college faculty because the teaching portion of the scholar's work was now of very minor importance. The professor could spend most of his time in Washington as an adviser to some federal bureau and return every now and then to the college to deliver an occasional lecture; he might even have his lectures read by an assistant.

Did the college object that he was neglecting his work and his students? Hardly. For to go to Washington as an expert also conferred prestige. Nor did the federal bureau or commission that requisitioned the scholar hide his light under a bushel. On the contrary, they publicized it widely to indicate that they were making use of the best talent available. And because his objectivity was assumed, it suggested that they were not motivated by partisan considerations in their decisions.

The president of the large corporation who engaged the services of a professor of psychology to develop personality tests for his executives, or the book club that engaged a professor of English as an editor or a member of their board of advisers, was similarly motivated. As far as the college was concerned, an advisory position with one of the giant corporations was as prestigious as one with the government. As far as the professor was concerned, it meant extra money. Not infrequently, he made more money from the textbooks he wrote and forced on his classes than he received for teaching the course, and by issuing frequent new editions he was able to prevent royalties from drying up through the resale of the books secondhand to the succeeding classes. Some professors, not satisfied with consultant fees and research grants, have even formed their own corporations and gone into business while retaining their connection with the college.

However, when you leave the academic cloister for the world and the marketplace, you take on the attitudes of the world and the marketplace. This has been clearly apparent in the political behavior of the professoriat during the last few years. When the Kennedy administration began to call upon large numbers of academic people, largely from the colleges of the Northeastern part of the country, it was soon realized that the President had not only enlisted experts to help the federal government, but that he had also quickly converted them to partisans of his administration. How could it be otherwise? They had been inured to the idea of spending their lives in a college community, politicking to be appointed to an important faculty committee, maneuvering for departmental influence and power, glorying in the mention of their names in a footnote in a learned paper. And suddenly they were called by the most puissant lord of the Western world to help him make decisions that would affect the lives of millions of people for decades and centuries. Their names would be mentioned in *histories,* not just in footnotes. Whole chapters would be written on their influence and importance. They would be the subjects of doctoral dissertations. It was heady wine!

When the assassination of President Kennedy brought Lyndon Johnson to power, the academic community reacted, not as though awakened from a pleasant dream by the rude clamor of the alarm clock, to yawn regretfully and wash and dress and breakfast and then go on to their regular jobs, but rather with the petulant indignation of a child being dragged away from the playground by his mother. What could they expect from a man who came from Texas and slurred his suffixes and had a wife named Lady Bird and had spent the greater part of his political life whispering in congressional corridors?

Where were the historians and professors of Government to point out that a man who had been Democratic Majority Leader during a Republican administration, who had been in a position to scotch all its legislative proposals, but instead had helped pass them, could be no mere party hack?

Their patron had been defeated even in his attempt to push a tax cut through the Congress. But when his successor managed to get one liberal bill after another passed, the professional historians regarded it as cynical hypocrisy on his part. These were liberal measures, and how could an oaf from Texas with an accent redolent of cowbarns and manure be a liberal?

When Johnson completed the unexpired term of his predecessor and was nominated for another term, tremendous political pressure was built up to force him to select Robert Kennedy as his running mate, even though it was common knowledge that the two men were not overfriendly. Apart from the dangers to the country inherent in such a situation, there were also questions of whether dynastic inheritance of power was in keeping with the American system, and even more whether a young man whose governmental experience had been as an assistant to Senator Joe McCarthy's notorious committee prior to his appointment by his brother to the post of Attorney General—"to give Bobby some experience before he opens his own office"—should be next in line for the Presidency of the United States. But the distinguished academic experts were as eager in pushing for the nomination as the most partisan politicos of the Irish Mafia.

It is understandable that the academic community should rally to the support of Senator Eugene McCarthy for his courage in challenging the President to bring an unpopular war to a conclusion. And his low-keyed and urbane speaking style was particularly ingratiating to the academic mind. What is less understandable is the failure of the professors to point out as his campaign continued that he wasn't saying anything. And what is even harder to understand is the cynicism with which a large portion of them threw him over as soon as Robert Kennedy entered the lists.

But perhaps the saddest view of the professor in politics was displayed when Hubert Humphrey was nominated for the Presidency. The two-party system is basic to our government. The voter is offered a choice of only two and he must choose the better, or even the lesser, of two evils. Never can he find a candidate and a platform that is exactly tailored to his requirements. For that matter, he can't in a multiparty system; he merely has a few more choices. On the other hand, the system insures stability and efficiency of operation, rather than the constant threat of collapse as in the coalition governments that are normal with the multiparty system. It works even if the platforms of the two parties are the same: Tweedledee out of office acts as watchdog and critic of Tweedledum in office. This is not a difficult principle to grasp, but it was evidently beyond the understanding of a large portion of the professoriat who reacted to the nomination by first petulantly announcing that they would not vote at all, then by announcing that they would vote for but not support Humphrey, and then that they would support him but not campaign for him. And when Nixon was elected, they wrung their hands and asked each other querulously what would happen to the country now.

Under the circumstances, one wonders if there might not be a conflict of interest here, easily as serious to the body politic as that which agitates the minds of the pundits about congressmen and judges. Psychiatry developed a profound credibility gap in the mind of the public when it was found that in every major murder trial where a plea of insanity was made both sides were able to muster psychiatrists of good professional standing to support their cases. Is not the situation very much the same today in the larger arena of politics where, on any question where expertise is involved, there are professors available to argue on either side?

In the light of the events of recent years, there is much to be said for the theory that scholars and professors don't belong in politics; it's strange country for them and they stumble and lose their way. By training they are more concerned with principles than with people. Their study has been of philosophical differences, of jesuitical hair-splitting differentiations between one school of thought and another. They have had few dealings with people other than their students, who are forced to listen while they lecture them. But government is the art of the possible, the art of compromise, and compromise means both sides yielding a little on their principles so that action can be taken that will be beneficial to both. Men of affairs understand this since they have been doing it all their lives. But the scholar regards yielding on a principle as unprincipled. He can function when his party has a large majority, but even then, because principles are so much more important than people to him, he tends to be ruthless and rides roughshod over any opposition. When he is opposed by a large and powerful minority, he is completely incapacitated.

But the political behavior of the professoriat raises another question: In the light of their partisanship, with its concomitant exaggeration of all that favors their side and equally exaggerated disparagement of all that favors the other side, can we be sure that in their published researches and in their doctoral dissertations they weighed the available facts dispassionately and objectively? Can we be sure that the facts that were contrary to the conclusion they were trying to prove were not swept under the rug and the figures that supported their conclusions might not have been stretched? And if they differentiate between their political methods and the methods they use in scholarly works, are the students aware of it? And do they make the necessary allowances? Or do they assume that one is just about as objective as the other?

CHAPTER 16

The Conspiracy

Well, by dint of hard work and with the cooperation of his father on the math assignments and of his mother in keeping his kid brother Dalton out of his way while he was studying, our Claude managed to gain admission to Prestige U. By the end of his sophomore year he sensed that this brave new world of college that he had worked so hard to attain was not all that it was cracked up to be. He couldn't tell his folks about it when he came home for vacation because they had worked too hard to get him in and were now working too hard to keep him there. He felt guilty about it, and his guilt manifested itself in a kind of abruptness and taciturnity in his dealing with them. And this made him feel even more guilty, of course, when he saw their hurt. He would have liked to drop out, maybe for a year, and just bum around or maybe get a job and then see if he wanted to go back. But that was out of the question because of the draft.

Perhaps if he had done better in his freshman year, gotten a really good running start, he would have done better in his sophomore year and felt better about the work in general. He had worked hard and had passed all his courses, even got a B in one course and a B minus in another, but he knew his parents were disappointed. His father had tried to conceal his disappointment. "That's not too bad," he had said. "Freshman year is always the hardest. But you've got to buckle down and work a little harder."

"Gee, Dad, I spent most of my free time studying."

"Well, you've got to learn *how* to study. That's the trouble with this high school here; they don't teach you *how* to study. I think the prep schools do a better job of it." It was his favorite criticism of the local school. He was convinced that there was a special trick to the business of study, like maybe this new fast-reading technique. Of course, Claude knew the real reason for his mediocre grades. He had been one of the bright boys in the high school and his marks had reflected it, but here all his classmates were the bright boys of their respective schools and the competition was devastating. Besides it wasn't just a matter of getting the work done; it was that they were all in competition with each other. If he wrote a very good examination paper, which showed that he had done all the required work and understood it, but someone else wrote a paper that the instructor judged better, then as the grade of his competitor rose, his accordingly dropped. So to get high grades, he not only had to do good work but better work than the rest.

Claude did not take a year off of course, but continued and finally two years later, graduated *cum laude*. His parents made a big thing out of it, but actually at Prestige U. many students graduate *cum laude;* at least a *magna* is necessary for real distinction.

At this point it might be worthwhile to listen in on a wildly improbable conversation between Claude and the dean of the college. I picture it as taking place right after the commencement exercises, when the proud parents are standing around sipping lukewarm punch and talking with those members of the faculty who have been induced to march in the academic procession and have been urged to circulate among the guests afterward.

Claude managed to get separated from his parents and finds himself standing beside the dean, who is also momentarily alone. If a Broadway producer is interested in expanding the ensuing bit of dialogue into a full-length play, we could give it greater plausibility by hinting early in the first act that a disgruntled member of the psychology department, passed over for promotion, had liberally laced the punch with truth serum.

DEAN (*Fanning himself with his mortarboard*). It's a nice day for it.

CLAUDE. Yes, sir. Sure is.

DEAN. And what are your plans for next year?

CLAUDE. I'm going on for the Doctor's degree—in English. I've just been accepted at Smarkatch State Graduate School of Arts and Sciences.

DEAN. And a very fair school it is. The English department has a very decent reputation.

CLAUDE. I was hoping to get in the graduate school here, but I was turned down.

DEAN (*The punch beginning to get to him*). Well, sure, Bub. You don't expect us to take in every Tom, Dick, and Harry that mooches in off the street.

CLAUDE. I didn't mooch in off the street. I just graduated from here. (*pointing to his gown*) Didn't you notice? I figured after all the money I paid in —

DEAN. Money *you* paid. Why every dollar you paid in tuition, we planked down five. Do you have any idea of what we pay out in salaries?

CLAUDE. I don't think it could be very much. This teacher I had in Economics A, a Chinese, he had a hole in his pants.

DEAN. Chinese? That would be Professor Svolitch's assistant. He was just poor-mouthing, looking for a raise. I'll fix his wagon at the next faculty meeting. But take Svolitch's salary—

CLAUDE. But he didn't teach the course. He was down in Washington all the time.

DEAN. Well, sure. That shows you the type man we have on our faculty. The government needed him. You don't expect a man like that to waste his time explaining the law of diminishing returns to freshmen. You understand it, don't you?

CLAUDE. Oh, sure. That's where if you got something like a bunch of apples—

DEAN. Oranges, boy, oranges.

CLAUDE. All right, oranges. So you like the first one, and the second is *comme ci, comme ça,* and the third one you could do without. After that you don't even want to look at them.

DEAN. See? You've got it. We teach you things here, boy.

CLAUDE. Well, there's this guy I know, a friend of mine. We went to high together. He went to State U. and he got the same thing in his class in economics.

DEAN. Well, that shows we're not teaching you wrong.

CLAUDE. But tuition only cost him a couple of hundred a year.

DEAN. But you were getting it from Professor Svolitch, straight from the horse's mouth. And if you wanted to check on it, you could go to the library, one of the best in the country. Four million books. Let me tell you that costs a pretty penny to keep up, and we keep it up for you.

CLAUDE. Gosh, I never got to use more than a couple of dozen books maybe in any one year.

DEAN (*growing manic*). Look, Buster, you're a big boy. Nobody had to put them in your hands. They were there for you to use.

CLAUDE. Well, gee, I wanted to, but I was kept so busy reading stuff for my courses and writing papers, I never had much time to read.

DEAN. And how about our museums and laboratories? How about our anthropology expedition in the Gobi Desert?

How about our astronomy observatory in South Africa? How about—

CLAUDE. I didn't get to use those either. None of the students did that I know of. At least no classmates of mine went to Africa or to the Gobi Desert.

DEAN. I should hope not.

CLAUDE. Then why did we have to pay for them?

DEAN. You one of those SDS types? Look, I'll tell you why you have to pay for it. That's what makes a university great, and you get the advantage of it, so that's why you have to pay for it. You were sniveling about Professor Svolitch not teaching you. What do you think you would have heard if he did? Bells ringing? It was his course in eonomics that you took and that's what the record says. That's why we pay him such a big salary. And the bigger he is, the bigger you are, so we don't waste his time having him teach you, but let him concentrate on writing books and serving on commissions in Washington.

CLAUDE. But it costs such an awful lot. My mother had to go back to work and my old man had to moonlight.

DEAN. What would they have done if they hadn't? Your mother would have busied herself with charities and organizations just to make the time pass. Well, this is an organization and a charity, too. So she worked for us indirectly. And what would your father do with his evenings if he weren't working? Watching television until he fell asleep, probably. Well, wasn't this better for him? And think how proud they were, lording it over their friends and neighbors because they had a son at Prestige. Look at it as a kind of initiation. You join a fraternity and there's a period when they make you do all kinds of foolish, undignified things that prove absolutely nothing. But when it's over, you're a member and you can enjoy all their social functions, the use of the house, of their dining facilities, all the rest of it. Well, think of the college as a kind of initiation. And as far as you're concerned, when you go job hunting next week, you'll find that being a graduate of Prestige opens doors for you that are closed to your friend from State.

CLAUDE. I'm not going to work. I'm going to graduate school. Remember?

DEAN. So you are. I forgot. Then you're going to be one of us. So there's no harm in telling you. You'll find it out for yourself sooner or later anyway. But if I tell you now, it will make the whole arrangement clear to you. Now listen carefully: It's all for us—the whole setup, the whole system—it's for us.

CLAUDE. I don't get it. What's all for us?

DEAN (*impatiently*). The whole college system. It's for us, for the faculty, not for the students. You'll get your Ph.D. one of these days and after a while you'll get to be a professor someplace. You'll work little more than half the year, what with vacations and exam periods and reading periods, and you'll teach maybe nine hours a week. As you grow, you'll get more money and even less work—six hours a week, three hours a week, maybe no teaching at all if you get big enough. Nobody watching you, nobody supervising you, nobody checking up on you. You want to take a trip to the big city, you just post a notice saying you won't meet your classes Thursday and Friday. And all the time people call you Professor and are respectful. When you want to sound off, you've got your classes—a captive audience, and young so they're easily impressed. And the big shots, the politicians, and the big industrialists they're impressed, too. They figure you're the one that knows. It's the most wonderful job in the world, I tell you. And all these lovely buildings, and this tree-shaded campus; all of it, it's all for us. Now do you understand?

CLAUDE. Do you mean that there's a conspiracy?

DEAN (*testily*). We don't all huddle together in smoke-filled rooms once a year, if that's what you mean. But we've got things nicely organized nevertheless, so that nothing happens on the academic scene, no change in organization, curriculum, or method occurs that doesn't make life easier or pleasanter for the professor.

CLAUDE. Like what?

DEAN. Well, like there's more and more emphasis on having students work on their own on major research projects, instead of frittering their time away in formal classwork. Whether they get anything out of it or not, one thing is sure—the professor will have a lower class load.

CLAUDE. Yeah, but how about all the preparation for lectures, and reading and marking papers? There's a lot more work to lecturing in class than just standing up and talking for the hour.

DEAN. A professor has to be pretty small potatoes these days if he does his own exam reading. He has assistants to do that for him. And as for preparing his lectures, why should anybody who has been lecturing on Chaucer or Shakespeare for half a dozen years have to do any work preparing his lectures? What new discoveries would have the slightest effect on what he said last year on the subject, or the year before?

CLAUDE (*suspiciously*). Why are you telling me all this?

DEAN. Because you're going to be one of us—one of these days —in five or six years maybe—and, and—I don't really know. (*Uncertainly*) Say, did you notice anything funny in the taste of that punch?

CURTAIN

CHAPTER 17

The Graduate School

It would be pleasant to be able to report that once having gained the rarefied atmosphere of the graduate school, our young Prestige U. graduate could finally relax. Unfortunately, the truth is that compared to the graduate school, the liberal arts college and all that went before is mere child's play. It is in the graduate school that the real competition is seen, for here the student presumably feels that he is drawing near the ultimate goal. In sight at last is the payoff that would make it all worthwhile—the job or the career.

Formerly, the law student looked forward to graduating, passing the bar examination, and then opening his own office; or if that were too hazardous, he could take desk space in an already established law office with some arrangement for sharing the expenses of the telephone and the stenographer. Fortunate was the young lawyer who was able through his father's business friends to establish a connection with an insurance company that would give him an occasional accident case, or with a real estate firm that would call on him now and then to do a title search. It took care of his office expenses and cigarette money until such time as he was able to build up a clientele on his own, usually through contacts made by joining a church and a number of fraternal organizations. One's parents were expected to help out. It was a rare parent indeed who on making a new acquaintance did not mention that his son had now opened a law office and that he would appreciate it if he kept him in mind when he needed a lawyer, simultaneously pressing his son's professional card on him.

Similarly, the medical student expected to hang up his shingle immediately after he had completed his internship. The great majority, if they thought of specialization at all, thought of it as something they would work into gradually in the future. They knew that their practice for the first few years would consist largely of treating colds, stomachaches, and cut fingers, that the work day would be long and that many of their patients would not pay; but usually it added up to a living that would improve as they became better known.

In recent years, however, establishing oneself on the small entrepreneurial level has become less desirable. Law students are less inclined to open an office immediately on passing the bar exam and look rather for salaried jobs with large law firms or corporations or for clerkships with important judges. They go in for specialities that call for advanced degrees, and for teaching in law schools that can lead to more ambitious careers. In order to qualify for these, merely passing their courses and examinations is not enough; they must stand high in their classes. To select the members for Law Review and Legal Aid, and to indicate standing in class, most law schools use a grading system as exact as that of West Point and Annapolis where it serves a similar purpose. In some schools, indeed, the averages are worked out to four decimal places.

And in medical school, as well, standing in class has great significance. There are not only preferred internships, but also research opportunities and positions in famous clinics. The number of general practitioners has dropped to the point where any number of rural communities are without medical service of any kind.

So the rat race goes on, more phrenetically than ever in the professional school. And is it to be supposed that the habits and mental attitudes of a lifetime will change after the last course and the last exam have been taken? It would be a miracle if it did, and it doesn't. In the hospitals, in the large law offices, in the great corporations, the competitive struggle goes on. But because the apparatus of examinations and grades is missing, it is done by scheming and conniving, by bootlicking and toadying to the senior executive, by elbowing and tripping one's competitor, so that one may gain the next rung of the ladder.

It is no different in the graduate school of arts and sciences than it is in the professional schools. Here, marks are of no great significance since the usual passing grade is B, and much of the work is on an individual basis. The competition here is for the favor of the one or two members of the department who have the greatest influence. These are the ones whose patronage means fellowships and assistantships, and eventual faculty positions at prestige colleges. The common method is to select a subject for the doctoral dissertation in the specialty of the professor whom you want to impress, and then to arrange to do it under his supervision. Or if the student has had some previous contact with the professor, he may hint that he would like to write his dissertation under his guidance and ask his mentor if he has any suggestions for a thesis subject. This is more flattering to the sensibilities of the professor, but it carries with it the danger that it is difficult to refuse the subject he might suggest.

The Ph.D. dissertation is the crowning indignity in the long initiation that eventually leads to a position on a college faculty. In the humanities it takes a minimum of two years and is at least as long as the average published book. But I have known graduate students who have been at the project for as long as six years and the end not in sight. Inasmuch as the dissertation must cover material not previously investigated and in this sense be an original contribution to knowledge, and inasmuch as thousands of dissertations are written every year throughout the world, it follows that most of them all deal with matters of such minor interest and importance as to be not worth the doing. And of course, as the number of dissertations grows, the situation gets worse from year to year. As matters stand now, it is questionable whether 90 percent of the dissertations written are worth the time spent on them. And this raises a further question: If the dissertation is written willingly, does it not automatically convict the candidate of lacking a sense of proportion, and hence of pedantry? And if it is undertaken unwillingly and only because it is a requirement for teaching in a college, can these two or more years of full-time devotion to a subject that an intelligent and reasonable man would not spend two weeks on fail to have a deleterious effect on the candidate's mental development?

There might be some justification for the system if the young doctor were subsequently hired to teach in the general area of the subject of his dissertation. If, for example, he had written a biography of an obscure eighteenth-century poet and were hired to teach eighteenth-century literature, it could be argued that even though his dissertation had been limited to the life of a single, very minor poet whose work was of little consequence, nevertheless his peripheral research would have given him an insight and feeling for the period that he would not otherwise have had. But as often as not, he will be teaching general survey courses and maybe even Freshman English for years before the opportunity arises for him to give a course in his special field.

But the system persists, in part because it is traditional, and in part because like the thinking that maintained freshman hazing for years in all colleges and still does in many, each generation of professors remembers how they felt about it, and sees no reason why the succeeding generation should have it any easier. In any case, this formidable hurdle limits the numbers in the exalted ranks and restricts the special perquisites to a comparative few.

But if the dissertation system is of no use in the practice of the profession of teaching, and because of its built-in pedantry does not serve to train the researcher in the intelligent discrimination and judgment required in true research, what else can it be but a form of initiation—like wearing foolish hats and singing songs on command from atop the library steps? One utility it does have: it separates the pliable, the obedient, the submissive—in short, the safe—from the bolder and more independent spirits who might kick over the traces; it is a screening device for maintaining the docility of the herd.

If we follow our young friend Claude through the course, we will see how the system works. It will be remembered that he failed to gain admittance to the graduate school at Prestige U., but had been accepted at Smarkatch State. Smarkatch was a relatively new college, founded in the twentieth century, and there were still bare patches on the gothic walls which the ivy had not yet covered. Although he expected he would be required to take some courses, he assumed that most of his work would be individual research under supervision. He found, to his surprise, that in his first year, he was not even permitted to take a seminar course, and that it would not be until his third year, at the earliest, that he would be able to make a start on his dissertation.

He also expected to have an easy time of it because of the difference in standards between Prestige and Smarkatch. In this, too, he was disappointed. The work at Smarkatch was much the same as the work at Prestige, and he discovered that the members of the faculty were likely to have academic backgrounds on a par with the men on the Prestige faculty. Indeed, they were not above commenting disparagingly on the scholarship of some of the most venerated names at Prestige. Perhaps it was just as well that he was not permitted to work by himself for the first two years; it took him almost all that time to disabuse himself of any fancied superiority of his Prestige degree and to learn about the cliques in the faculty so that he could eventually decide which to join for the better chance of advancement.

There is an intra- as well as an interdepartmental pecking order. In the field of English, status usually is in the order of the antiquity of the specialization, so that the Old Englishmen and the Middle Englishmen and the Chaucerians stand at the head of the list, followed in turn by the Elizabethans, the post-Elizabethans, and eighteenth-century men, and the Victorians. The Contemporary Literature men have the lowest status. After all, what is scholarly about reading stuff that other people read for pleasure?

Once he learned his way around, the problem of picking a man was not too difficult for Claude. Professor Guildenstern, who taught Philology and Old English, was the chairman and obviously the most powerful man in the department. But he was within a few years of retirement and hence was something of a lame duck. Professor Rosencrantz, the Chaucerian, was new to the department and did not get along well with Guildenstern. To work with him might be interpreted as being anti-Guildenstern, and there was also a strong possibility that he might soon move on to another post; he was reputed to have friends in the state legislature.

Professor Arundel, the Elizabethan expert, was in his late forties; he was a reputable scholar in good standing with the administration, and with many connections with English departments in other colleges. He would normally have been Claude's first choice. However, he was a martinet and a slave driver. To do one's thesis under his direction meant delaying one's degree by a year or two. His graduate assistants complained that they had to do so much of his work that they had very little time for their own.

The eighteenth-century man, Malachy Moviss, had personal problems. He was a balding, youngish man, abnormally sensitive, and constantly suffered from wholly imaginary slights at the hands of his colleagues, his students, the administration—almost anyone. Claude had taken a course with him and found him uncomfortable to be with.

Which left Morton Merton, who taught Victorian literature.

Professor Merton, a machine who ground out paper after paper for the learned journals, ran his classes with clockwork precision. His notes were complete and in order and he never deviated from them. He knew exactly how much ground he would cover in each lecture and he permitted nothing, neither question nor discussion, to interfere with his goal. One joke he permitted himself, in his first lecture, and then it was all strictly business. "There is apt to be some confusion about my name," he would say. "It is Merton Morton—I mean, Morton Merton." When the laughter subsided he would continue. "In any case, my initials are M. M. If you have occasion to leave something for me in the English office, and are momentarily confused—and you see it is quite possible—[sycophantic chuckling and gurglings from the students] please do not try to dodge the difficulty by addressing it to M. M. There is another member of the department with the same initials and we must never confuse the eighteenth century with the age of Victoria." (Renewed laughter.)

So Claude, having taken his course in Dickens and Thackeray the first year, registered for his course in Tennyson and Browning the second year. And in his third year requested permission to do a research project under Merton's supervision, which hopefully would develop into a doctoral dissertation.

The topics Claude suggested were dismissed out of hand—one as being too inconsequential even for a doctoral dissertation, another because it covered too much ground and would take years to cover completely, the third because it would be sure to involve material that had already been done.

"Do you have any suggestions, sir?"

"It so happens I've got just the thing. It's a subject I was planning to work up myself for a paper for the PMLA, but I don't see my way clear to getting to it in the foreseeable future, so there's no reason why you can't do it. There was a minor poet, a very minor poet, I might say, around the turn of the century—one Simeon Suggs. Ever hear of him? No, I shouldn't think you had. He wrote some doggerel—none of it good, but he was a clerk in a publishing house and that brought him in contact with all the big writers of the day. There are some letters and there is a diary that I came across in the British Museum that you can arrange to have Xeroxed and sent to you."

Claude would have preferred to work on something more promising, but it was evident that Merton was interested in this project and it would be impolitic to the point of folly to turn it down, especially since there were several other graduate students trying to curry the professor's favor.

When he finally began work on the project, it appeared even more futile than he had feared. What little of Suggs's verse had appeared in print had obviously been used as filler material for a weekly that the publishing house had embarked on. The magazine had run for a few short months and then abruptly suspended publication. Suggs's extant letters were all to his wife on the occasion of her having gone to spend some time with an uncle in Manchester, and except for a few scattered references to people who had come to the office on business, only served to emphasize the dullness of the inconsequential Suggs. The diary was of a piece with the letters and there was nothing in either of them to explain why they had not been used all these years to start a fire in the grate.

There were occasional verses in the diary, and references to others which he had written in public houses and restaurants when in his cups, presumably on the backs of old letters or on scraps of paper or on tablecloths or on the tables themselves. He seems to have been a compulsive rhymer when he'd had a drink or two. And there were tantalizing references to names more familiar—"Saw Bennett [Arnold?] at the Dog and Shield and he was . . . !" or "Galsworthy in this morning and very much as usual." But nowhere was there a description of Galsworthy to indicate what Suggs might have regarded as "usual."

There were times when Claude despaired and wanted to give it all up and start on a new subject; there were times, when, because of his concentration, the subject assumed an importance and magnitude that surpassed all the major writers of the period. But he persevered and little by little the work progressed. In his fourth year he was appointed assistant in the Browning and

Tennyson course. The work consisted of grading papers, keeping records of student grades, explaining exam marks to students who were sure their work had been underrated, and helping his mentor with his research by checking details, copy-reading, and typing his manuscripts. There was always the delicious possibility that if Professor Merton got sick, he might be asked to take over the class during his absence, but the opportunity never came. Professor Merton remained disgustingly healthy. All in all, it was a lot of work, but it meant some money in his pocket. More, it meant that he had won the confidence of his mentor. Unfortunately, another graduate student, his rival in Professor Merton's interest, was appointed to assist in the Dickens and Thackeray course.

Both men got their degrees the following year. There was a vacancy on the faculty and both were hoping for it, but it fell to one of Guildenstern's protégés. Professor Merton, however, came down handsomely with a fine letter of recommendation, ". . . one of the brightest young men who has come under my hands in recent years. His thesis, *The Life and Writings of Simeon Suggs,* a real contribution, was considered for publication by the university press and only lack of funds . . . He has a flair for research and would make a superior teacher. . . ."

At Brannue U. where Claude was hired with the rank of assistant professor ("State regulation, you know. Two years' experience required for the rank of associate"), he gave a course in Freshman English ("All our new teachers take a turn at Freshman English"), two sections of a survey course in English literature, and a course in contemporary drama for a total teaching load of twelve hours. It was four years before he was made an associate professor—budget troubles after the two-year minimum—and was able to drop his Freshman English course. Although disgruntled by Merton's failure to secure him an appointment at Smarkatch he kept in touch with him, and when he polished up a course paper he had done some years before, he sent it to him for comment. Through Merton's good offices he was able to get it published in the PMLA.

By the time he became full professor, five years later, he was *the* Victorian expert in the department, his teaching load had been cut to six hours, and he was now more concerned with supervising the work of graduate students than he was with lecturing. As one of the faculty members on the board of the university press, he was able at last to get his doctoral thesis published in book form. A full professorship when he was still in his thirties automatically stamped him as brilliant and the fact of the publication of his thesis constituted automatic proof. But more, it proved that he knew his way around in faculty politics, and hence was a good man to know. *He* was now courted by graduate students with an eye on the main chance, and several of them found themselves surprisingly interested in the contribution of Simeon Suggs to the development of Victorian poetry. In fact, one of his students, with the aid of the university computer, found some very surprising correlations between the frequency of use of certain words in Suggs and of the same words in the poetry of John Masefield, suggesting a hitherto unsuspected influence of the one on the other.

The real high point of his academic career, however, came when he was on a sabbatical in England. He was taking a walking tour through the Lake District and stopped at a small inn for lunch. Afterward, he retired to the privy for postprandial elimination and meditation. Being a compulsive reader, and having neglected to take a book or newspaper along, he found himself reading the graffiti on the marble slab that separated his section from the adjoining pew. There were the usual lewd line drawings and obscenities, but then as his eyes grew accustomed to the dim light, he noticed what appeared to be a longish poem of some dozen quatrains, barely discernible, although evidently written with a particularly penetrating indelible pencil. He could make out only a line here and there, but at the end the poet had signed it with his initials, "S. S.," surprisingly clearly, because he had gone over them several times and then decorated them with flourishes.

It came to Claude in an intuitive flash that this was nothing less than an original poem by Simeon Suggs. And no sooner had the thought struck him than confirmatory evidence suggested itself to his scholar's mind. Several times in the diary Suggs had mentioned lunching on bread and cheese at a pub and the first couple of lines of the poem were

> A lunch of bread and cheese and beer
> Delighted the heart ere I came here.

Also in one of the letters to his wife, he had mentioned a proposed company picnic. It could have been here in the Lake Country. Lines for investigation raced through Claude's mind. He could check the files of the local paper to see if the picnic had actually taken place. Perhaps there was a reference in the files of the local constabulary. Some of the old codgers in the town might even remember it.

Claude had intended to press on after lunch, but now he decided to stay a few days. It turned out that there was no local newspaper, and the local codgers had no memory of so commonplace an event, which presumably had happened half a century earlier; all except one, a very old man, who responded with "Ay, Ay" to all questions put to him. Nevertheless, Claude did uncover evidence that he felt no reasonable man could reject. In the old account books of the inn, which he persuaded the innkeeper to dig out, there was an entry showing unusually large receipts for the day, with a curt notation in a spidery hand, "city folk." By collating the date of the entry in the account book with references in the diary to the purchase of a new boater, presumably for the coming day in the country, Claude felt that he had irrefutable and conclusive proof.

In an essay that he wrote for the *Lamplighter,* the Brannue U. student publication, when he resumed his classes in the fall, Claude recounted not only the story of his hectic pursuit of evidence—the triumph of nailing down a fact, the heartbreak of following a clue only to have it lead nowhere—but also the negotiations he carried on with the Brannue U. Library Committee to authorize the purchase and to appropriate the necessary funds.

He did not mention the efforts of the physics department and the chemistry department, the one by the use of X rays and infrared photography and the other by the use of chemicals to render visible those portions of the poem that had been all but obliterated by time, because that occurred sometime after the slab was delivered to the university. But the president in his speech accepting the slab for permanent display in the college library spoke of it. He characterized it as "a fine instance of interdepartmental cooperation" and summarized the whole affair as "a thrilling example of the romance of research, another adventurous step in Man's long march to Truth."

Unanimity, however, is rare in scholarship and there are cynics in Academe as there are elsewhere. Even in the English department at Brannue there were invidious remarks to the effect that the poem wasn't worth spoiling a perfectly good privy for.

Of greater importance was the suggestion of a scholar from the state college that the "S. S." stood for Sacheveral Smith, a poetaster of the period who had lived for some years in that area and who was known to have actually frequented that very inn. Not only did our hero join battle, but several of his former students, now teaching on various college faculties, came to his defense, as did, of course, graduate students who were now working for their degrees under him. The Simeon Suggs-Sacheveral Smith battle raged for months but it is generally agreed that Simeon Suggs forces finally got the better of it. One result was that the Simeon Suggs forces formed an association called the Simeon Suggs Association, which was intended for the gathering and discussion of Suggsiana, and the publication of a journal that would incorporate and publish the latest scholarly developments in the field. Needless to say, all graduate students working in the Victorian period at Brannue joined the association and paid the ten-dollar membership fee. A couple of years later, a student was awarded the doctorate for a dissertation on "Reconstruction of the Inn Poem and the Suggs-Smith Controversy." The following year, Claude brought out a textbook for the survey course in English literature, and although there was some grumbling from the publisher, he managed to include several poems by Suggs as well as excerpts from the diary and the letters.

CHAPTER 18

The Answer

We are now in a position to discuss and perhaps to answer the questions raised in Chapter 1. It is the seeming irrationality of the student strikes and rebellions that is disturbing. They are irrational in that they are wildly exaggerated responses to relatively minor faults—if faults they are—in the present college situation. They are irrational in that those who are involved, young people of middle-class background, have seemingly the most to gain from the college and the most to lose if their rebellion leads to expulsion. They are also irrational in the way in which they are conducted: not by pointing out the evil and asking to have the matter corrected, but by demanding that the change be made instanter and declaring that the matter is non-negotiable.

On occasion the demands were presented in the form of an ultimatum—with a time limit. Sometimes the sit-in or demonstration came first and the explanation and the accompanying demands came later. Frequently, when the demands were acceded to, a new and enlarged set of demands was immediately trotted up as though the rebellious students were determined to find something the administration could not swallow, like a bully determined to pick a fight. As often as not the demands were impossible to fulfill.

Although there are dozens of strikes, sit-ins, and demonstrations going on in colleges across the country for dozens of different reasons, there are nevertheless trends or styles in student rebellion. At one time, the fashion was to give sanctuary to an army deserter, and no student body could consider itself socially conscious unless they had a deserter stowed away somewhere on the campus, usually in the chapel, and usually chained to the lectern or at least to a slew of students who volunteered for the duty. When the army came to claim their own, sometimes the students were able to mount a sizable opposition, forcing the authorities to elaborate stratagems to spirit the prisoner away. Sometimes he surrendered meekly and subsequently made a statement to the press expressing his regret at the trouble he had caused the military authorities and his determination to accept his punishment in a soldierly manner and finish out his time afterward. His erstwhile student supporters regarded this as the result of a brainwashing by the army, or the response to a promise of lighter penalties if he made the statement. And it may be so, but it could also be that after a few nights of sleeping on the floor of the chapel and meals of sandwiches and lukewarm coffee, the army stockade may have seemed a milder form of punishment. For those who wondered how the soldier happened to come to the college in the first place, a degree of enlightenment was offered by students at a local college who demanded that the administration give sanctuary to a soldier even before one had applied. They explained that they would have one as soon as the local committee that supplied them had one available.

The fashion recently has been to focus on the ROTC, and

college faculties and administrations have suddenly discovered—after forty years in some cases—that the course in military science is either not in keeping with liberal arts study or that it does not measure up to the academic standards of the college. The unseemly haste with which the colleges accede to the demands of the student activists suggests that either the college has been one of the most unfair and repressive institutions in our society or else that the professoriat is a timid, rabbity lot, fearful and yielding to any pressure group whether it be the government as in the days of Senator Joe McCarthy, or the administration, or the alumni, or the student body. It suggests that those few student activists who are political anarchists and who really want to destroy our society show a tactical wisdom far beyond their years in beginning their attack on its soft underbelly, the college.

But of course, the true political anarchists are only the handful on each campus who start a sit-in campaign or a strike. The several hundred that follow them are quite ordinary politically, not revolutionaries or hoodlums, but rather middle-class children of middle-class parents, law-abiding and intelligent. What leads them to engage in these undemocratic, antisocial, and frequently illegal escapades?

Let us hear from Dalton, Claude's kid brother, on the subject. Dalton is an undergraduate and, although not a member of SDS, is very much involved in the student militancy at his college.

"Because I've been gypped. That's why. I've been played for a sucker. . . . How? Well, let me tell you. All my life, all I ever heard was Prestige U. My old man went there for a couple of years on the GI Bill after he got out of the army. He never graduated, see, beause he met my mother and decided to get married and go to work. In those days you did that, I guess, when you got married. I mean, you didn't finish out school while your wife worked. Crazy! But I guess it was different in those days. You could get a job even without a degree. Maybe if he had finished, things would have been different around here. I mean, college wouldn't have been such a big deal to him.

"But as it was, college, especially Prestige, the way he talked about it you'd think it was heaven. His being a lot older than a lot of the guys may have had something to do with it, having been through the war and all. Anyway, Prestige was the whole world to him. When there was company over, he'd manage to drag it in that he was an old Prestige man. And when he'd get a letter from there—you know, asking for a contribution or something like that—he'd always make a point of opening and reading his letters on the train, instead of at breakfast, so the guy sitting next to him could see it. Get it?

"Well, he kept after my brother Claude, and when Claude made it, he was so proud, you'd think Claude had just been elected President or something. Claude was a brain, though. I mean right now, he's a big-shot professor at a college out West, and he's written a book and everything. And let me tell you, it wasn't easy for my folks, I mean moneywise. My old man got this job in the evening where he goes out and gets answers to questionnaires. And my mother went back to work, too. She used to be a secretary to this big-shot manufacturer. I was pretty grown-up by that time, I mean, she didn't have to worry about me coming home from school and her not being there.

"So then he started in on me, not that I hadn't had it right along; just that he'd been concentrating on Claude. But once Claude was in, then it was my turn. Except that I didn't get the marks Claude got. I mean, he was a brain. I liked to read and all that, but I really had a tough time with my math, and that being my old man's specialty, he'd get all uptight about me not digging it. So that made it a lot harder for me than it had been for Claude. And of course, I always had Claude thrown up to me.

"To tell the truth, I wasn't too keen on going to Prestige. I'd just as soon have gone to the state college. A lot of the kids I rocked around with went there and tuition was only two hundred a year. I figured if they got me a car, I could even live at home and it would cost practically nothing. But when I hinted at it once, my old man got on his high horse. 'Now you let me worry about the expenses, young man. That's my responsibility.' That kind of crap. This was right after I got my marks in the Boards.

I'd done all right in the Verbal, even better than Claude had done, but the Math wasn't so hot.

"Well, by some miracle, I got in. And I guess it wasn't such a miracle. I mean, I did get this high mark on the Verbal. And then the dean of admissions was this guy that Claude had been at Prestige with, and of course, I'd given his name for reference, and I was like a legatee at that. Still, I would rather have gone to State, because you know what my old man went and did? He took a mortgage on the house that was practically all paid for. And this other job that he'd had—I knew he would have liked to give that up because it was pretty tiring going to see people in the evening after he'd done a full day's work, but of course he couldn't what with the tuition fees and board and lodging at Prestige.

"Well, first semester, it wasn't so bad. I mean I was away from home for one thing, and I had a lot of free time. I mean, it wasn't like nine to two-thirty like in high school, and teachers checking to see if you did your homework every day, and detention if you didn't. You only have to go when you've got a class, see, and I was taking four courses, so the most I'd have in any one day was three lectures. And you could take five cuts in any one course. Upperclassmen could take as many as they liked. So I took it easy. I'd feel kind of guilty sometimes when I'd think of my folks working so hard to pay for it, but once on vacation when I suggested that maybe I ought to switch to State for the next year, my old man blew his stack. So I didn't talk about it anymore. I mean, what are you going to do with a guy like that?

"All my instructors that first semester were young guys, and they were all right, but I couldn't see that they were all that wonderful. I mean I couldn't see how they'd be so much better than instructors someplace else, like State, for instance.

"But second semester I got to take a course with one of those big-shot professors. He wasn't very old, but he was all bald, and he had these thick glasses and was always kind of smiling like he was pretty pleased with himself. I didn't think so much of him. He was always talking about himself, about what he said to this guy in the government and about what the Secretary of Agriculture said to him. He'd never have enough material to finish the hour, so he'd always end early by saying something like that was all the pearls he had to scatter for that day. And every time, about half the class would laugh or kind of snicker like it was a good joke. It was pretty sickening.

"And do you know what I was paying for those lectures? Ten bucks apiece. Look, from the first of October to the middle of May, that's seven and a half months or thirty weeks. So take off three weeks' worth of vacations and a couple of weeks each semester for exams and then a couple of weeks for a reading period, and you find there are only about twenty weeks' worth of lectures. So in a three-hour course there are sixty lectures. Now I pay twenty-four hundred a year for tuition, so that means six hundred dollars per course because you only take four courses. So is that ten bucks a lecture or isn't it? And when this guy decided to post a notice that he won't meet his classes next week on account he's going to Washington to testify before some committee, it's still ten bucks apiece for the lectures we don't even get.

"Now get this: I'm taking this Freshman English course and it costs the same money. So I was listening to a couple of seniors talking in the cafeteria, and they're talking about the young guy that's giving my section of Freshman English. He's a teaching fellow and he teaches two sections of Freshman English. And you know what he gets for it? Twenty-five hundred dollars. That's what he gets for teaching those two sections, and there's thirty kids in each. That's sixty kids and at six hundred smackers apiece, it brings in thirty-six thousand dollars. For thirty-six thousand that they get in, they pay out twenty-five hundred.

"Let me tell you, by the middle of my sophomore year I was pretty disenchanted. I couldn't see that I was getting anything very much. I had one guy who wrote the textbook we were using in the course, and all he did was lecture from his own book. And then there was this course where it was mostly discussion, but if you tried to talk to any of the guys outside of class, about the course stuff, I mean, they'd clam up. They were all afraid that something they'd say, you might use in the classroom and then you'd get the credit. And then I had this guy who was always telling stories about the writers we were studying, little anecdotes that were interesting enough, I suppose, but I couldn't see that I was learning anything that I couldn't get by myself, and I got the impression that he was telling us those stories just to show us how much he knew. And to add insult to injury, you had so much reading to do, and course papers, and getting ready for quizzes that you never had any real time for yourself.

"Maybe it was because I was in a field like English literature. Now you take my roommate; he was in chemistry. He looked at things a lot differently. For one thing, he was getting facts, you know what I mean? It wasn't just a bunch of opinions like I was getting in my courses. The stuff I was getting, I could get on my own just by going to the public library, but the stuff he was getting he had to get in college. I mean, most of it was lab work, and there are no free labs around, if you see what I mean.

"And those profs—you couldn't talk to them like after class. They were always in a hurry. They'd finish their lecture and they'd scoot off like a sheriff was after them or something. You sort of got the idea that teaching us wasn't their job at all, just something they had to do to draw their pay.

"Well, like I said, by midyears in my sophomore year, I was able to see how things stood and that I'd been had. But what are you going to do? I couldn't talk to my old man about it. Once, when I complained about the work, he acted like I was ungrateful for all he was doing for me, and that it was only my fault and I wasn't taking advantage of my cultural opportunities and all that crap.

"Actually, though, my sophomore year was a lot more fun than freshman year because I'd made some new friends. They were a lot more easy-going than the guys I knew at first. They didn't bother about clothes and they'd let their hair grow long partly because they couldn't bother cutting it and partly because it bothered the jocks and the ROTC boys and the other good citizens of the college. There was this apartment where this graduate student Joe lived with his chick, and let me tell you, she wasn't loose or anything like that. As a matter of fact, Edie was one smart gal, and talked just like a man. Most of the chicks that used to hang around there were the same way. You'd drop in there of an evening, and there were always a bunch of guys around, and you'd sit around and just shoot the breeze. Maybe listen to some records, or sometimes a guy would have a guitar and would sing folk songs, and we'd have some drinks. It was nice. I mean these guys were bright. Every one of them was a brain in his own way, and they were from all the colleges around. I got to hanging around there a lot.

"Sometimes they smoked pot, and at first that made me a little uncomfortable. I tried it once, but it didn't do anything for me, so I didn't bother with it. I never saw anyone get really lit up from it, so I guess it's like a lot of other things you're told. They just ain't so. But, like I said, it didn't do anything for me, so I didn't mess with it.

"Some of these guys were in English like me, a couple of them doing graduate work in the field. Boy, they knew about these profs. There wasn't one of them they could agree on was any good. And then there were some people in economics and some in government. And there were a couple of psych majors and this graduate student in philosophy that when he talked, everyone would listen. He's going to be a real biggie someday, I'll bet. And that was another thing, these seniors and graduate students, didn't look down their noses at you because you were only a sophomore.

"When I first came to school, I had all these clothes that my folks had gone and bought me. You know, regular suits and sport jackets and slacks. But then I began to dress like the others—just comfortable. These blue jeans with flannel lining—they're warm in cold weather. And you don't have to worry are they pressed or anything. And this blue denim jacket—let me tell you it's the most comfortable jacket I ever had. And when it's real cold, you wear a heavy turtleneck underneath and you're comfortable and warm in any kind of weather. And I let my beard grow just for the hell of it to see what I'd look like. It kind of itched at first, but after a while you get used to it, especially if you don't think about it. And when you'd walk down the street, especially when you went into town, people would look at you and sometimes you'd hear them say 'hippie' and you'd get stubborn about it and it made you feel that you were doing what you liked instead of what they thought you ought to do. And do you know, you saved a lot of time not shaving or bothering about clothes. And another thing, maybe it was just a coincidence, but I found I was making out better with the chicks.

"I'd been pissed off with my old man since the last time I was home, and every letter I got, especially when my grades dropped a little at midyears, I got more uptight about. So in a way I guess a lot of this business of letting my hair grow and my beard and wearing these clothes was like doing the opposite of what he expected me to do. And then I got to feeling that where he was so all hepped up about what he was doing for me, and about outfitting me, this way at least I wasn't wearing his clothes. Do you get the idea? It got almost like a game. I'd think what would he expect me to do, and then I'd just do the opposite. Once I didn't shower for over a week just because he was always talking about how important it was to be clean.

"April vacation I was going home and I thought I'd better shave and get my hair cut before leaving because I knew they'd have a fit if they saw me. But then, I got another letter from my old man and it was about some TV show he saw, a documentary on colleges, and how he hoped I was keeping good company and not getting involved with 'these crazy hippies' and I got plenty burned about it. Parents! That was another thing about this gang I was going with. They said just what they thought, and some of the things they'd say about their folks—well, it kind of shocked me at first. One of them happened to say his old man was a bastard, for instance. And then I got to thinking about it, and I decided that maybe my old man was a bit of a bastard, too.

So I thought I wouldn't bother to change, and let them see me as I am.

"You can imagine what my mother said when she saw me. She didn't know what to start on first, my long hair or my beard or my clothes. She finally let up on the clothes because I didn't have anything else to wear anyhow. I mean, I'd left all my good clothes back at school. But she wouldn't let up on the hair and the beard, and she kept making sarcastic remarks. But when the old man got home, he really had a fit. One thing led to another and we had a regular row, and finally I said, 'All right, if that's the way you feel about it, I'll quit school.' And do you know—that stopped him. He was scared. He was real scared. He didn't say another word. He just left the room. Can you imagine? He was scared I might quit school. When I went up to bed, their room was dark but I could hear them talking. And they kept on talking until I fell asleep. And they didn't bug me for the rest of the time I was home.

"I didn't see much of them except around dinnertime. That was the only time we were together, because I got up after the old man had left and they'd both be gone for lunch. But when we'd talk at the dinner table, he'd say something, and I'd contradict him if I felt like it, and we'd argue a little and then he'd just listen. I think maybe the beard had something to do with it. See, he being clean shaven, the beard made me look older. So maybe he felt that it wasn't like talking to a kid anymore. He'd go out in the evening for this other job he had, but Saturday night he didn't work, of course, and usually they'd go out for a ride and maybe an ice cream. But this Saturday I had a date and I asked him for the keys to the car, and he just handed them over without a word. Let me tell you, that was pretty unusual, but he was scared to cross me; he was real scared I might quit school.

"I don't mind telling you when the vacation was over I felt pretty high all the way back to school. I must have looked like an idiot in the bus because I kept grinning to myself every time I'd think about it, about me and the old man, I mean. It was the first time I'd ever stood up to him.

"I got back, and another first happens. I went to this apartment I told you about, Joe and Edie's, in the evening and along about midnight when I'm ready to go back to the dorm, Joe asks me if I'd take this chick Laura home. There was a lot of talk in the newspapers about a guy breaking into girls' apartments, and she was a little scared. So, although it was late, what could I say except OK? So we had to take the streetcar and what with waiting around, by the time we got to her place, it was pretty late. And I was wondering if I could get a streetcar back or would I have to hoof it, two or three miles.

"She said there was one more car but it wouldn't be along for a half hour or so. They don't travel regular at that hour. So I went up to her place to pass the time a little because it was kind of chilly out. Well, we're sitting around smoking and talking. We don't really have too much to say to each other. She's a senior at this girl's college and she's in math and I'm in English lit so what is there to talk about? And then she goes to the window and she looks out and says 'I'm afraid you missed your car. It just went by. I'm sorry.' So I says, 'Well, I guess I better get started.' So she says, 'You can stay over here, if you like.' So even then I didn't tumble. I figured there was another room and another bed but I'm a little excited anyway. So I said, 'Gee, thanks. That's swell.' So then she says, 'It's pretty late. I think I'll hit the sack.' And she takes off her sweater and she doesn't have anything on underneath except this little bra.

"So, I didn't know what to do. I mean, it wasn't as if I'd ever made a pass at her. I'd seen her a few times up at the apartment, but she was pretty quiet and didn't talk much. I didn't know whether to make a wisecrack or to go over to her and start petting her. So I played it cool. I started to undress. She doesn't say a word but goes right on undressing. She wiggles out of her slacks and then out of these little silk pants and then she says, 'I always sleep in the raw,' and she slides under the covers just like we'd been married twenty years. So I said, 'I do too,' and I finished undressing and I got in beside her. She snicks off the light and says good night and turns her back to me. Well, I was green, but I knew that was an act, so I pulled her toward me and turned her around and we started loving each other. And then afterward we just went to sleep.

"The next morning, she's up first and she's in a housecoat and she's making breakfast. She asks me if I got anything I got to do and I tell her I had a class. So she says why don't I cut it. I thought she wanted us to hang around all day, and to tell the truth I just wasn't anxious. But she says there's this guy recruiting seniors for jobs with this chemical company and a bunch of kids are planning to put on a demonstration because they make this napalm that's being used in Vietnam. Well, you know there'd been a lot of talk around campus about this because it had happened at another college, and I didn't like the idea of a company manufacturing napalm, but then I wasn't crazy about guns and ammunition in general, and I couldn't see much difference in being killed one way or the other. I mean the thing itself is neutral, it's the people who use it that are right or wrong. Then again, this outfit was one of these giant corporations and this napalm business was just a tiny fraction of all the stuff they make and sell. What's more, I couldn't see how we could stop them from recruiting. They could always do their interviewing in a hotel room if they wanted. But I figured the demonstration might be some fun, so I said, 'Sure, I'll go along.' I didn't tell her why I was going because there's one thing about this chick—she's all serious. No humor whatsoever, just a hundred percent serious.

"Well, it *was* fun, at least for the few hours I was there. We sat in the corridor of this wing of the administration building and we barred the door to the room where the interviewers were so nobody could get in and the interviewers couldn't get out. Nothing much happened while I was there, except a bunch of jocks, mostly football players, tried to break through. There was some pushing and some punches were thrown, but our side didn't give way, and then the dean came along and told the jocks to leave. I guess he didn't want a riot. I mean, he wasn't on our side, believe me. We just sat around and talked and sang. It was a regular party but I left around noon because I had this class that I didn't want to miss. Laura stayed, though. She told me later she stayed till midnight when the interviewers were rescued by the campus cops through the window with a ladder.

"The next morning, she calls me and do I want to go to a party and if I want to I can stay over at her place again. So I said OK. I had this paper I had to write, but I figured I could work on it over the weekend. Well, this turned out to be a grass party. Most of them, like the chick, were getting through that year, or they were in graduate school. There were even a couple of instructors, Ph.D.'s. I tried the stuff again but I didn't care for it. I didn't notice that it did anything for Laura either. I mean she didn't talk much before, and she didn't afterward. We called this Gus's place like the other place was Edie's place. It was a different gang, though, that hung out here. They were all terribly serious about everything. They were always going on about The Establishment. At first, I thought a lot of it was hogwash. I mean, for crissake, like it was a worldwide organization like in these spy pictures, deciding on every little thing like the war in Vietnam and on birth control and fluoridation and pot. You'd think they were against anything that could make things easier for people just because they wanted to be cussed. I never argued with them because I was so much younger than most of them and they were all so sure of themselves and had figures and historical parallels. But I'd argue some with Laura when we were alone at her place.

"Sometimes we'd go there and sometimes we'd go to Edie's place. Things were easier at Edie's place. The gang there was more interested in music and poetry and painting, and you could have a few laughs there. I'd always suggest we go to Edie's place, and she'd always suggest we go to Gus's place. I guess most of the time we went to Gus's place, and after a while I kind of got into their ways of looking at things. And do you know, a lot of it wasn't hogwash at all.

"The chick graduated in June and went home to the West Coast right afterward. Her folks came on for graduation so I didn't see her for those last few days and I never had a chance to say good-bye to her. I didn't hear from her until almost a year later when I got this wedding announcement. I thought maybe

I ought to send her something, but I was kind of short at the time and I never got around to it. Then I met this girl that came from her home town and knew her, and she said the guy she married was an accountant. Can you imagine, an accountant? To tell the truth, I wasn't sorry that she left. She wasn't a very good-looking girl, but like they say, what a build! But what I objected to was she was so damn serious all the time. I mean you couldn't kid with her; she was so sensitive. And you couldn't even talk with her much. When I'd stay at her place, if we got home early, she'd maybe fix some drinks and then we'd just sit around and sip at our drinks and maybe read the paper, just like an old married couple. Then she'd say that she thought she'd hit the sack and we'd go to bed. And you know, I don't think she was any more interested in me than I was in her.

"I got a job at school, in the library, for the summer, which was all right because I didn't want to go home. I mean hanging around a small town all summer long—that can be pretty grim. I'd get a job in the grocery store, maybe, and I'd probably have to shave to do that. So I decided to stay in town. Well, that was almost as grim. There was no one around except a bunch of schoolteachers taking summer courses. And it was hot as hell most of the time. I played tennis a little and went swimming once or twice, but most of the time I just vegetated.

"Then the fall term started and life was back to normal again. And suddenly, everybody is all uptight about the war. I mean, the guys at Gus's and at Edie's, the kind of guys I rocked around with, we were always against the war, of course. But we weren't really doing anything about it except talking. Somebody always had a clipping with them that he wanted to read about the war, and then we'd talk about it, but I guess we all felt it was like a tornado; you just had to wait it out. But then the casualties began to go up from a dozen or so a week to a couple of hundred or more. And those were deaths. The wounded were always about ten times that. That's really what started it off. Before that, there were always guys saying they were conscientious objectors and how they were going to jail rather than be drafted. And there were other guys who said that they weren't conscientious objectors, but they weren't going to fight in *this* war. There was all kinds of talk about going to Canada or England and asking for citizenship there. And some guys claimed they had ways of beating the physical. One guy said that if you acted queer and told the army psychiatrist you were homo, they'd let you go. But he was a homo anyway.

"But most of them chickened out when they were actually called. I saw this guy who'd done a lot of talking about going to Canada, and he'd been drafted and was home on leave before going into training. I asked him how come. And he said he'd had this long talk with his folks and decided that the easiest thing was to go in. There was a chance that he wouldn't go to Vietnam, for one thing. Maybe Germany or some other place in Europe. And he thought he had a good chance because his father knew somebody who he thought could fix it. And even if he went to Vietnam, well there was no real danger there. 'After all, when you consider there are only a couple of dozen casualties a week, it's as safe as living in New York.' That's where he came from—New York.

"I guess I felt that way, too. I mean, you go up to Canada, say, and you don't know anybody there and the chances are it wouldn't be easy getting a job. They'd think of you as a slacker and a draft dodger—the Canadians, I mean. What kind of job could you get? See what I mean? And if you refused to serve and went to jail, well you know, the poor slobs in jail, they're apt to be more gung ho than the Marines. You could get your brains beaten out, or worse. But then when the casualties jumped up to a couple of hundred, things began to look a lot different. A lot more guys, ordinary guys, and even some government biggies were talking against the war and saying we had no right to be there, and it was a war you couldn't win, and it was ridiculous all that money and lives just so's not to admit we made a mistake.

"The Student's League invited this guy to come down and give a talk about the war. He was going to talk in the auditorium, and it had been all set, all the arrangements made and everything. Then suddenly, the administration says he can't come. First, they say he can't use the auditorium, and then when the Student's League says, 'OK, so he'll speak at the student's lounge,' the administration says he can't come at all. Let me tell you, everybody got pretty damn hot about that.

"There was this instructor, an assistant professor really, who was practically a regular at Edie's. He claimed to have the low-down on the whole business. The college does a lot of work for the government, research, I mean, and it's a pretty good deal. The college gets a lot of dough and the profs that are involved get a pretty penny for their extra time. Well, according to him, the government had hinted that they didn't want this guy to talk, and that they might pull out of this research agreement they had with the college, so that was why the administration had banned him. According to him, there were plenty of guys on the faculty who would side with the students if they pulled off this protest march that was being planned.

"So the Student's League announced a meeting to discuss the situation. Their idea was to pass a bunch of resolutions that would be presented to the administration, and see if they couldn't arrange for a meeting with the board of trustees on account it was a serious infringement of academic liberty. Well, that meeting didn't go off the way it was planned. I don't think anybody had any idea that it would work out the way it did. First, a lot of guys came down to the meeting with these picket signs. And they were what you might call restive. See, the guys that run the Student's League, they were all for doing things orderly. They wanted to pass this resolution. Then they'd appoint an ad hoc committee to meet with the trustees and explain their position. Nothing was said about what would happen if the trustees didn't want to see them, or if they did and just turned them down. So there was a lot of booing from this bunch with the picket signs, and after a while, more and more guys began to side with them.

"We were all kind of excited, see. And then somebody yells out, 'To hell with a committee, let's go down to the administration building right now, and tell them what we want.' Well, you never saw anything like it. Everybody was yelling and offering his two cents' worth, and the chairman was rapping away with his gavel just making more noise, and everybody was arguing with the guy next to him. And all this time, there were photographers from the newspapers popping off flashbulbs and taking pictures like crazy.

"So then somebody yells, 'Let's go,' and a bunch start moving for the exits. Well, some guys thought we should stay and do it legal and proper, and not get stampeded by the radical element. But then we see that the photographers are moving to the exits and a lot figured they'd go along because that was where the action was going to be. I don't know, maybe half the audience starts moving out. This guy I met down at Edie's, he sees me and hands me a picket sign and I find myself right up there with the leaders.

"Everybody is yelling and waving their picket signs and those that didn't have them were holding up their fingers in a V, like V for Victory, and other guys are marching along with their arms up in the air and their fists clenched. Then four or five guys begin chanting, 'Hell no, we won't go,' and pretty soon everybody takes it up and we're yelling it in unison and kind of marching in time to it, and these photographers are running ahead and turning and snapping pictures like crazy.

"We march right up the steps of the administration building and then right up to the second floor where the president has an office and also the dean. There's this old biddy at the information desk on the first floor and she's kind of bleating, 'You can't go upstairs without an appointment', and 'I'll have to ask you to leave.' Then somebody pushes her desk back so she's kind of caught in her swivel chair between the wall and the desk and she can't get out. But she continues yelling at us and waving her pencil at us. The other clerks were kind of frightened, and the girl at the switchboard was talking into her phone, calling the campus police, I suppose.

"Upstairs, there's this cool blonde Katie Gibbs type and she says, 'The president is out of town.' So we tell her we'll talk to the dean and she says the dean is at a meeting. So then somebody says, 'OK, we'll wait until he comes back,' and a bunch just plunk themselves right down on the floor. So there we are, a bunch sitting on the floor, and a regular mob surging up the stairs. And when they find there's no place to go, they sit down on the stairs. So then this Katie Gibbs type says, 'I don't believe the dean will be back today,' and we tell her that it's all right, we'll wait until he does get back. So she says, 'Very well,' and she gets up and takes her purse like she's going to the can. And that's the last we ever see of her.

"Nobody tried to stop her or anything. It was all good-natured. We were having a ball. From what I heard afterward, the girls downstairs, including the old biddy at the information desk, left about the same time. The campus cops came and asked us to leave, but they must've been told not to get tough, because after a while they just went away. There were students milling around outside by the hundreds, sometimes chanting, 'Hell no, we won't go,' but most of the time just standing around and talking in small groups. We were looking out the window and they'd wave to us and we'd wave back. Sometimes an argument would get started and a crowd of fifty or more would gather and from upstairs we could see the couple of guys in the middle, arguing and waving their hands, and then the crowd around them would move away and cluster someplace else.

"Because I was in the office, that made me one of the leaders kind of. We talked about what we ought to do off and on. Some of the guys were worried that we might get suspended or even expelled, but most of the time we weren't worried. There was so many of us, see. I mean, they couldn't expel half the school. Originally, we went just to see the president or the dean, but when they weren't there, our idea was to stay until five o'clock and then leave. But then we decided, Hell, why not stay there all night? The only problem was food. So we took up a collection to send someone out to get sandwiches and coffee. But before we could send someone out, food began to be passed up to us from outside. A lot of the guys had been yelling down to the guys outside, 'How about getting us some sandwiches and coffee?' and they had passed the hat around outside.

"It was no sweat staying the night. Most of the time we talked and sang and argued. Then when you got tired, you just sacked out on the floor. The next morning, the dean and a couple of the office help came down to go to work like nothing happened. Well, we had discussed it, I mean what we were going to do, and when he came to the door, we told him we weren't going to open up until we'd seen Prex. So he tells us that he's on the West Coast and we just say, all right, we'll wait. He tells us that our actions are illegal and that we are in danger of expulsion and all that crap, but then he goes away. The fact is, he didn't know just what to do. There were a lot of faculty on our side, which made it even tougher for him. He was afraid to call in the city police because there's always been bad blood between the school and the city government and between the kids and the cops. And once the cops were allowed on campus, there was no knowing what would happen.

"It surprised me about the faculty, though. I would have thought that they'd all be on the side of the administration, and of course a good portion of them were. But then in talking it over, we decided that there was a split in the faculty, and that the young ones would naturally be on our side. You take these Teaching Fellows for instance, I don't suppose they were too happy at the deal they were getting. And then even the regular ones, the young assistant professors, and those who weren't on tenure, life wasn't too easy for them at the college, either. They were always being goosed to publish and were always in danger of losing their jobs. And then there were some who felt that canceling the lecturer was a blow to freedom of speech and academic freedom and all the rest of it. In general, it was the old geezers who were with the administration and the young ones who were with us.

"Well, you know what happened: we were there a whole week, and then Prex arranged to meet with a committee of students and faculty and they decided to let our lecturer talk provided there would be someone there to speak for the other side after he was finished, that that was the right democratic way. So the question of discipline of the students in the administration building came up, and Prex allowed how under the circumstances they would overlook it. So we came out. Actually, a lot of the guys had left at various times during the week, because they had work to do at the library, or maybe just to get a decent meal and take a bath and change their clothes. Some had come back, and some new ones, but some that left never did come back.

"In a way, the whole thing was a bust, because when that lecturer came, it was one of those nights when it was raining cats and dogs and we didn't even fill the auditorium. Then he turned out to be something of a dud. Maybe this was the first time he was speaking at a college and he thought he ought to speak nice and proper and he was just dull. People began to leave before he was finished. Then when the other guy got up, the speaker for the other side, practically everybody left except a small bunch that just kept chanting and yelling so you couldn't hear him.

"I went home for the April vacation and my brother Claude was there. He'd come East to show off this chick he was going to marry. She's all right, I guess. I mean, she's like working for her doctorate in sociology, but she was kind of stiff all the time like she had a tight girdle on. You know what I mean? My brother Claude, though, he'd changed. He must've put on thirty pounds since the last time I saw him a couple of years ago. And he was all palsy with the old man. I mean, whenever there was any kind of argument or discussion, like after dinner, he'd always side with the old man. Like when we talked about the riot at Prestige. Naturally, the old man thought it was terrible. I mean, that's the generation gap. He went on about how it was all the work of a handful of Commies and how they had influenced the rest of us. I didn't say anything at first because you couldn't convince him about anything once he'd made up his mind, and, besides, Claude's girl was there and I didn't want to start a family argument in front of her. I mean, the old man can get really worked up. But then Claude said he didn't mind orderly protest, but he thought it was 'reprehensible'—that was the word he used—to break a bunch of furniture and this computer that the administration claimed we'd wrecked.

"Well, you know that computer—none of us guys who were in the office on the second floor knew about that till afterward. See, the computer room is down in the basement and it wasn't as though we in the office were in command. I mean, there were guys all over the place and no one was giving orders or anything like that—and no one was taking them either. Now and then, someone would make a suggestion—you know, 'Let's do this,' and then someone would say, 'Nah, the hell with it,' and then we wouldn't.

"And to tell the truth, when I heard about it, I felt a little funny. I mean, sitting in is one thing, but breaking up stuff—and that computer was supposed to be worth, well I've heard as high as half a million. We talked about it at Edie's one night and this guy said it reminded him of the time he went to this expensive restaurant where they practically charged you for a glass of water. He didn't mind too much because he was promoting this chick and he wanted to show her that nothing was too good for her. But then the food turned out to be lousy and there wasn't even enough of it, and he felt gypped. He felt like busting up the joint, but of course he didn't dare. But then the chick got her dress caught in the tablecloth and all the dishes slid onto the floor. Of course he made a show of being awfully sorry, but inside he felt real good because he'd got a little of his own back.

"This guy at Edie's said breaking up the stuff at the college was like that. Well, I didn't buy it at the time, but seeing Claude sitting there, puffing at his cigar and being so goddam cool and know-it-all—that got to me. So I said, 'Why in hell not? Why ever in hell not? Look at all the dough we pay into the college and what we get for it. A couple of my profs haven't even been there half the time. And when they are there, they just go through the motions.'

"So my old man says, '*I'm* paying for it. You haven't contributed a thin dime for your education.'

" 'Oh, sure,' I says, 'you pay for it by working at two jobs and by Mom working, and by mortgaging the house. But you don't hide it from me. You let me know about it all right. And you don't think that's payment? And how about the four years of my life? You planning to take care of that, too? You go into a store where they overcharge you, and you're damn sore about it. Maybe you don't do anything about it except make up your mind to go someplace else. But what do you do about it if there is no other place, or if you find out all the other places are in cahoots and are doing the same thing? At first, maybe you just grouse, but when there's no improvement, you feel like wrecking the place.'

"So Claude, he takes a delicate puff on his cigar and he says kind of dreamily, 'I remember what my old economics prof, the great Svolitch, used to say in that connection, Dalt. According to him, from an economic point of view, it didn't make any difference. If everybody thought you did, then you still got value for your money. It was like a fraternity initiation. The things they made you do, didn't do you any good, but it was only after you'd done them that you could become a member and go to the dances and use the frat house. Same way with college. Maybe the courses don't do you any good, but it's only after you've passed them and gotten your degree that you can get a decent job and live a decent life.'

"So then I got good and sore and I started yelling. 'That's a crock of shit! Maybe that's the way it was in your day and that's why you guys stood for it, but they've raised the ante since then. Nowadays, when you graduate, you don't step into a good job, or go to graduate school either. Instead, they grab you and ship you over to Vietnam where a couple of hundred are killed off every week and maybe ten times as many get wounded and spend the rest of their lives dying. Maybe those who come back whole can get started on that good job, but a lot never get it. Well, it's too goddam much; the odds ain't worth it.'

"Well, that broke it. Everybody started yelling, but mostly my old man. How he wouldn't tolerate that kind of language in the presence of the ladies at his own dinner table and then he went on about my clothes and my beard and beatniks and hippies and drugs—you name it. What can you expect? I try to tell him why we had this riot, and all he can think of is my language isn't refined and there are ladies present as though they're not people.

"Then I got caught up in this McCarthy business. I didn't really think he was all that big, but I was getting near draft time, and here was a regular senator who was saying we ought to get out of the war, so naturally I was going to back him. I didn't figure he had a chance, but I thought if we made a lot of noise, it might help things all round. I even went up to New Hampshire when he went up there to campaign. I didn't go ringing bells, on account I wouldn't shave my beard, but I worked in the office mailing stuff out mostly. There were these two chicks in the office with me, and we'd sit around and talk a lot. One of them was named Bella and the other Stella, Stella and Bella. When I wanted to talk to the two of them—I was like office manager for a while—I'd call them Stellabella like it was one name.

"This Bella, her voice would get sort of hushed whenever she spoke of the senator. I asked her once why she was up here working like a dog when she must know he didn't have a chance. She got real mad at me. She said he was the most wonderful man she had ever met. He was like Jesus, she said. Can you imagine that? A real kook. Or maybe she hadn't met too many men; she was a mess. This Stella was a lot smarter. She said she had come up here because she was plain sick of school and wanted a vacation. Her folks were liberal types, who'd raise the roof if she goofed off, but this way it was all right because it showed she had social consciousness.

"McCarthy won big in New Hampshire and everybody was sure it was straight to the White House for him. That's all they talked about up at Edie's was McCarthy, and how wonderful he was. All except one guy who used to hang around there a lot. I never knew his real name because everybody always called him Diogenes. And you only had to be with him for a little while to see why. That guy didn't believe in nothing and nobody. He was the most cynical, pessimistic guy I ever met. When they'd start talking about McCarthy, he'd always interrupt with something like, 'Well, tell me just how he's going to stop the war? What you're all afraid to say is that the only way is to surrender. And he's afraid to say it, too.' But it didn't make any difference who you mentioned, he'd always have a criticism. Lyndon Johnson, Stokely Carmichael, Martin Luther King, Che Guevara —it didn't make any difference who you mentioned, he was down on all of them. I always figured he was a kind of nut. There were plenty of them that wandered up to Edie's.

"Then when Robert Kennedy announced that he was going to run for the nomination, about half the gang at Edie's switched over right away. Boy, there were arguments about that. The McCarthy people called the others traitors, and the Kennedy people said they were just being realistic, that Kennedy had a chance and McCarthy didn't, and that if Kennedy got in, they'd be in a position to take over. I happened to leave one night the same time Diogenes did and we walked along together. He wasn't talking, so after a while I said to him, 'What do you think of the gang being able to take over if Kennedy should get it?' He laughs and then he says, 'Did you think because they talk so high and idealistic, they stop being human? They're still people; that's something they can't escape.' So I asked him what's the answer and he says, 'I think maybe another flood with power transferred to some other species maybe.'

"Of course I figure him for another kook, but there's one thing you got to say about guys who don't believe in anything: they're usually not afraid of anything, either. Every now and then, there'd be some black guys up at Edie's. Everybody was so anxious to treat them equal that it always ended up with their being more equal than anybody else, if you know what I mean. Most of them would just sit around and talk like everybody else, but every now and then you'd get one that was full of beans. He'd accuse everybody of being a racist, and there'd be a kind of chorus of everybody admitting they were, but each claiming they realized it and were trying to work out of it. But Diogenes wasn't having any. He just said, 'You guys are the worst racists of all. You treat your own worse than any white Southerner ever treated you. And if things had been the other way, you would have dealt with the whites as bad as they ever dealt with you, or worse. And all this new cant about how it's all the white man's fault and how much better you are and how black is beautiful—you're kidding yourselves the same way your grandfathers did when they told themselves they were going to go to heaven. When you're poor and miserable, refusing to face reality is one luxury you can't afford.' So the black guy blustered some and said Diogenes talked like a typical racist. And Diogenes says, 'Racist? You bet I am, but it's the human race I'm against, not just yours.'

"Another time this black guy was telling us about a sit-in they were having at this college and what they were demanding, like an African studies course with a black director that they'd choose, more black students and black teachers, a black student lounge—the usual. When he got through reading off this manifesto, Diogenes said, 'I'll bet I know what's eating you guys: for half of you it's a cop-out; you can't do the work and you don't like to admit it. But all of you have the idea that if the college gives you something, it's like charity, but if you demand it and put on a big stink about it and the college yields, then it's like you got it on your own.'

"I didn't go to the Chicago convention like a lot of the guys did. To tell the truth, what this guy Diogenes said kept getting to me. I don't know what to do. Sometimes I think maybe the thing to do is to just do nothing, just kind of bum around, you know, not get tied up with anybody, with a gang or a movement, but just live from day to day and when I get tired of one place, move on to someplace else. Then I think maybe I should plan on going to another country, say like India and maybe study with a guru. And then sometimes I think that the only intelligent thing to do is to go on with my schooling, then get a graduate degree of some kind and get on the gravy train myself."

CHAPTER 19

How to Change It

It was no accident that the student rebellions were coincident with the sudden increase in the war effort. I do not suggest that the protests and the sit-downs and the demonstrations were motivated solely by reasons of personal safety—not that there would be anything wrong if they were—but it is easier to be idealistic about a new and better social order if one is personally endangered by the errors and faults of the old.

So the student lashed out at the war. But because he felt cheated he also demonstrated for all kinds of other causes that had no connection with the war. This intelligent, sensible scion of the respectable, hard-working, responsible middle class was ready and eager to fight for any cause, however minor or extravagant or downright impossible, that would embarrass "them," the Establishment, the oppressor, the enemy. Society, the Establishment, had arranged matters so that a college degree was necessary for a white collar job and then changed the college so that it gave nothing, no observable substantial benefit other than the degree, and then further arranged matters so that the degree no longer gave access to the job, but rather to service in an unpopular war that offered an excellent chance of being killed or permanently maimed. Like my grandchild, the student could not voice his real hurt, even if he could think it; he and his parents had too much invested to be willing to face up to the reality that the gilt-edged stocks they had purchased were no more than fancy, engraved paper.

So, again like Nina, he cried about old hurts, imaginary hurts, any hurt that the handful of revolutionaries on the campus could dream up. They responded eagerly to the most outrageous suggestion of the little handful of campus radicals, the same ones whom they had formerly jeered at as crackpots. Surprisingly, they were frequently seconded by members of the faculty. Usually, these were the younger men, the instructors and assistant professors, those without tenure, who also had grievances against the system; but occasionally some of the older men joined them; I suppose because in our youth-oriented society to be on the side of the young is to be with it, and to be on the other side is to be ready for the scrap heap.

All right, what can be done about it? And what promise does the future hold? Obviously, since the war in Vietnam is the immediate irritant, its termination will reduce much of the tension on the campus. Changes in the draft law could also ameliorate the situation. But neither the one nor the other, nor both in conjunction, will solve the problem, which is that, other than the actual degree, the college offers *nothing* that is remotely worth the time and money involved, and yet it is absolutely necessary for the kind of job that will offer a decent future.

Obviously a change is necessary, but because the faculty and administration have so large a vested interest in continuing along present lines, no radical change is likely to come from the college itself. What has in effect happened to date has been that faculties and administrations have yielded to student pressure on peripheral demands that do not get at the heart of the problem and, even more important, do not threaten the privileges and perquisites of the members of the club. With many a peccavi and mea culpa, in an effort to put a good face on it, they agree to an Institute of African Studies, to increasing the influence of the student in academic decisions, to a relaxation of dormitory rules, to almost anything except what is basic and significant. "You want a course in Swahili? Why, sure. Funny, how we didn't think of it ourselves. Sorry."

"You'd like us to sell our war industry stock? You're absolutely right. You see we bought these stocks when the companies involved were just manufacturing automobiles and fertilizers and things like that and we just kind of drifted along."

"You'd like to have co-ed dormitories with no supervision? Well, why not? I mean, you're mature enough to discipline yourselves, and if you're bound to do something—er—unwise, our watching you won't prevent it. That's my view of the matter."

"Degree credit for volunteer work in the slums? Splendid idea. Believe me, we're happy to see that your generation has developed a social consciousness."

"You'd like professors to meet all their classes and teach them personally? Well, now there, I'm afraid there are difficulties. I mean, if Professor Zilch, for example, is engaged in some delicate research problem, you wouldn't want him to drop his work and hurry to give a lecture, would you? I mean, he's engaged in searching for truth, you know, and that's what college is all about, isn't it? And Professor Pilch—when he's called down to Washington by the State Department, or even the President himself—you wouldn't want him to say he can't go because he's got a class to teach, now would you?"

Although the entire educational system from kindergarten to graduate school is out of phase, it is not necessary to restructure it in its entirety. The leverage of the liberal arts college is so great that if it were changed to conform to its original purpose and to serve its original function, the rest of the educational parade would fall into step. Once it was understood that the liberal arts college is not in essence a preparatory school for the professional schools, that it is not in essence a prerequisite for a job in corporate industry, that it is not a training school at all in the sense of providing an expertise in a particular field in the service of society, but rather an educational institution intended for the instruction of those who are interested in learning for learning's sake, then the system will straighten itself out by the internal logic of the concept.

Once we grasp this concept, it will become immediately apparent that our present system of admission by competitive examination is as pointless as it would be if applied to a hospital or a theater or a train. The candidate should be able to prove that he is capable of carrying on collegiate work, if only to prevent him from wasting his own time and money and to keep him from taking up the teacher's time to no purpose. Obviously, the kind of examination that suggests itself, nay that logic demands, is a comprehensive examination which would be marked on a straight pass-fail basis. It indicates purely and simply that the candidate either can or cannot carry on the work. Of course, there will be errors; any human testing device is bound to be imperfect. But the mistakes will be minimal, and for the ordinary student who has decided it is liberal arts study he wants, there should be neither for him nor his family any fear or tension.

And this in turn would have the effect of restructuring the system in the secondary school by removing the abnormal competition and the special devices that the secondary schools have incorporated in their curriculum in an effort to meet the unusual demands of the college. Who knows, it might even halt the flight from the city.

The same logic would suggest that the pass-fail system should apply in the college itself, because its goal is to broaden the mind of the student, to change him, and grading on a comparative scale for this is as senseless as grading for virtue. One immediate effect would be that the student would pace himself on the basis of his own needs and interests rather than to surpass his classmates. In other words, he would be properly motivated, and the correct motivation of learning for its own sake is essential to the liberal arts idea. Another effect would certainly be that the college would once again become a pleasant place instead of the torturous treadmill it is today.

Understanding the true function of the liberal arts college would also tend to return it to the students, not in the sense of our contemporary student activists who wish to control its administration, but in the sense of serving their needs rather than those of the faculty. Its basic function calls for it to be a place where students learn and teachers teach. If the teacher wants to do research, he should do it on his own time and for his own purpose, not for the honor and prestige of the institution. This would cut down a great deal on the scholarly publication that now practically engulfs us, and that would in itself be a good thing.

Ideally, the liberal arts college should be only for those who want to learn; it should not be a gateway, certainly not the only gateway, to the professional school. And this suggests that the professional school need not be a graduate school. The expertise of the present-day doctor is probably greater than that of his predecessors because of the great advances that have been made in medicine as in all sciences in recent years. But there is more than expertise involved in the practice of a profession. There are ethical considerations and dedication to the purpose of the profession. And it would be hard to prove that the caliber of the present generation of doctors and dentists and lawyers in these respects is greater than their predecessors under whom they studied, many of whom entered the professional school directly from high school. One might even speculate that the long and expensive preparation of four years of liberal arts study in addition to the three years of law school or the four years of medical school might lead to a greater interest in recovering their investment than in the ideals of the profession.

The development of our educational system over the years was not planned; like Topsy, it just grew. The rules governing the preparation for the learned profession were promulgated by the professional societies concerned and were intended at least in part to limit competition by making it difficult to gain the right to practice. In the light of the long opposition of the American Medical Association, for example, to the passage of the Medicare bill and to progressive legislation in general, can anyone believe that our doctors, in demanding so long a period of preparation, are inspired solely by the ideal of curing the sick, and not the least bit by the desire to protect their financial earnings? And can we assume that the legal profession is less venal?

There are graduate schools and undergraduate schools of education; there are graduate schools and undergraduate schools of business; schools of journalism, on the other hand, tend to be undergraduate institutions as do schools of engineering; there are two-year secretarial schools and four-year colleges of secretarial science offering a bachelor's degree; a similar situation prevails in the nursing profession. Why these differences? Because in general, when a professional group becomes strong enough, it lengthens the training period and raises the educational qualification for admission to restrict its membership. Conceivably, if the Newspaper Guild, for example, were to become strong enough, they could make of journalism a graduate study; and if they could, they would.

There is no reason to believe that a doctor or a lawyer whose training was purely professional and who never attended a college of liberal arts would be less skillful or less dedicated than one who did. He would merely be four years younger. If the additional four years of maturation are important, and they might be, the same effect could be achieved by raising the age limit for admission. While marking time, the prospective applicant could serve his hitch in the army, or go to work to earn his tuition money, or go to a four-year college of liberal arts. If his liberal arts study gave him an advantage that the others did not have, then their army service or years of work would give them an advantage that he would not have.

Again, one could argue that if the mental discipline derived from liberal arts study is useful in doing the work in the professional school, the mental training derived from the study of a profession would be similarly helpful in the liberal arts work and that it is just as logical to have liberal arts study come after professional study as the other way around.

Nor is it fanciful to assume that a move in this direction is impossible or even unlikely. A certain disenchantment has already set in with the protraction of medical study for example. To be sure, the longer the medical student spends in study, the more he knows; but on the other hand, the feeling is growing that as a result not enough medical care is being provided for the community. Some medical schools have taken cognizance of the problem and have been flirting with the idea of a shorter medical course.

Corporate industry's demand for a college degree as a prerequisite for executive training is perhaps a harder nut to crack, if only because it is even less logical. Frequently, the very men who demand it as a sine qua non for executive employment in their companies are themselves without college training. Nevertheless, they will no doubt continue to insist on a college degree, thereby maintaining the association of the liberal arts college with the good job. But here, too, there is the possibility of a change. The growing militancy of the black community has resulted in the opening of job opportunities to blacks which a few short years ago were unthinkable. In many cases, it is mere tokenism—with a Negro occupying a desk in the front office largely for show. But if it is felt that more is necessary, even if only for the sake of public relations, then jobs will be reexamined and reevaluated so that more blacks can be hired whose educational background is less than was formerly required. And if a job is reevaluated to permit the hiring of a black, sooner or later the same privilege and courtesy will be extended to the white applicant. It is fanciful, to be sure, but if the noncollege black can breach the walls to executive employment in corporate industry, he will be doing more for the black community—and the white—than anything the black militants on the campus could accomplish with their demands for African Studies programs and courses in Swahili.

Freeing the liberal arts college from its unfortunate relationship with the professional school and big business so that the high school graduate will have other paths open to his ambition will of course materially cut down the number who apply for admission. There will still remain, however, the problem of the prestige college with its unfortunate effect on the educational system. One solution would involve the recognition that in the prestige school nowadays it is the graduate school of arts and sciences rather than the undergraduate liberal arts college that is important. For some years now the tail has been wagging the dog.

The graduate school of arts and sciences is the one graduate school that must continue as a graduate school since it involves the continuation of the same studies that are taught in the liberal arts college. But it is in the graduate school that the great libraries and laboratories, which are mere prestige-adding items in the undergraduate college, become useful tools. The same is true of the famous scholars on the faculty; in the undergraduate college their expertise is perhaps wasted, but in the graduate school, dealing with embryo specialists in their respective fields, they could be truly useful, rather than as now parasitic on the liberal arts college.

Over the years, the prestige university has accumulated a vast collection of libraries, laboratories, and scholars of minimal use to the undergraduate, but essential to graduate study and research. So it would seem that if the university recognized the situation, it could with no great difficulty abolish the undergraduate liberal arts college and become a purely graduate institution. Its function then would be to turn out trained specialists and researchers for government and industry, and to train college teachers.

The first advantage would be a wholesome separation of the liberal arts function from the professional training function. More, the liberal arts undergraduate would not be subsidizing with his tuition fees that part of the university work from which he derives no benefit, and conceivably his fees might come down to more reasonable levels. Finally, the reputation of the undergraduate college would come as a result of the success with which it performed its essential function of educating its students, rather than through prestige by association with the research and discovery done in the graduate school.

What is it that we would accomplish? I envision a young man graduating from high school with a variety of choices open to him. He could take a job directly, without automatically setting a limit to his advancement. The fact that he had not gone to college would not pawn his future and restrict him to a kind of second-class citizenship. Or, he could elect to get into one of the professions without incurring the extra expense of four years of liberal arts study and could begin his practice at a younger age. Or, he might decide that since he now had a profession by which he could earn his living, he could afford to go to a liberal arts college in order to expand the range and interests of his mind.

Or he might decide to go to a liberal arts college first on graduating from high school. Then after getting his degree, he could decide whether to take a job in which his liberal arts study might counterbalance the experience on the job of those who had gone to work directly. Or he might elect to study one of the professions. Or he could decide to go on to graduate study in a particular field with a view either to college teaching or to scholarly research for the government or in a research and development program in private industry or as a member of the faculty of a graduate school. Whichever course he elects at the graduate school, it is hoped that in the restructured institution, he would not be forced into the futile exercise of writing a doctoral dissertation in order to get his degree.

If it is a college teaching career he is aiming for, then certainly it is pointless to require him to prove his capacity or ability as a researcher. One can be a scholar by virtue of knowing one's special field without doing research at all. On the other hand, if he is planning to make a career of research, some practice in it is obviously desirable. But there is no reason for this to take the form of the typical doctoral dissertation. It would be far better if he were directed to research a problem in his field, one of a list that his department had decided required investigation. Then he would not only get the research practice that would be useful to him in his future career, but would also make a valid contribution to the knowledge of the field. But I envision this as taking three or four months rather than three or four years.

Of course, so complete a restructuring of our educational system is not likely in the immediate future. Even if an earnest effort were made by the colleges themselves to change the present system, if only in the hope of stilling the clamor on the campus today, it would be done by committees of professors who are oriented to the general principles of the present system and have a vested interest in it; for that reason they could not recommend the radical changes that are necessary. They are products of the competitive system, and they approve of it because they have landed at the top of it.

They cannot see it as restrictive; they cannot see that it is a denial of the glorious capacity of the human mind to expand, to overcome all kinds of handicaps to attain its objectives, to grow as necessity demands. Our psychologists tell us that a person's I.Q. remains pretty much the same throughout his entire life. Our educators accept this and develop a system predicated on the basic assumption that the mental equipment you are born with determines the educational track on which you must ride and the level on which you must remain. For the top 2 or 3 percent, there is Prestige U.; for those less gifted, there is Smarkatch and Brannue and the two-year community college.

To all but the 2 or 3 percent, this is a stultifying doctrine that spreads tension and discontent and fear. It has resulted in setting up social levels that are a denial of democratic principles and that are all the worse for being unofficial and concealed. The fact is, and the examples are legion, that the mind even more than the body is capable of growth and expansion. The ninety-seven-pound weakling can and does become a muscled Atlas through desire and willpower and work, and the dullard can similarly achieve learning and develop wisdom of the highest order.

Now the key to the whole situation is the prestige college. Admission to it is presumed to indicate that one has a mind of the highest caliber, and graduation from it to indicate that one has reached the highest level of intellectual attainment. But although we have a test of a sort for the one, we have no test of the other. That is, although the College Board examinations and other bases for admission to Prestige U. do indeed tend to show that the students they admit are among the brightest academically, we have no proof whatsoever that the prestige college is indeed superior to the other colleges in the performance of its function. It is purely a matter of faith. And this is curious, since this presumed superiority is precisely why there is so much competition to get in, and is the reason for these bright young people selecting it in the first place.

What is even more curious is that we have no means of testing the efficiency of one college against another. There are no national standards, no national examinations, no national supervision. In the professions there are at least state board examinations, a bar examination for law and a state board exam for medicine and dentistry. And the various specialists in medicine all conduct examinations that the doctor must pass before he can be regarded as an accredited practitioner of the specialty. But there is nothing to indicate that an A.B. degree from Prestige calls for the same level of knowledge as the degree from Smarkatch or Brannue.

It would seem that a student getting an A.B. degree with a major in English from one college should have approximately the same amount of knowledge of the field as one getting it from another college. It would seem also that inasmuch as the government lists the A.B. degree as a requirement for some of their jobs that they would want to stipulate that the degree from one college should have approximately the same value as the degree from another. But there is no such stipulation. The matter could be readily decided by a comprehensive test just as it is in law and medicine, or, for that matter, as it is in granting admission to college. But there is no likelihood of the government's setting up such a test because of the hostility of the colleges to the slightest hint of government intrusion in their domain. There is even less likelihood that the colleges themselves would attempt to set up such a system of examinations.

As matters stand now, the American educational system is a hodgepodge, and the standing of the individual college and the consequent value of its degree depends on how well known the institution is—and this may depend on how successful its football team is. Even if the college is known for its faculty, there is no guarantee that this affects the instruction the student receives. So there is confusion and uncertainty and doubt, especially on the part of the student and his parents.

On a recent airplane trip, I fell into conversation with the young man sitting beside me. He told me he was a senior at college, and perhaps because he sensed that I was not too impressed when he mentioned the name of the school—I knew nothing of it—he added that it was the thirteenth largest school in the country. And before I could stop him he reached for his billfold and drew out a well-worn newspaper clipping that showed the standing of the largest colleges and pointed to the place his school occupied in the listing. It brought to mind an acquaintance whose son, having been turned down by the prestige colleges of the Northeast, had been admitted to a well-known college in the Midwest. He, too, carried a newspaper clipping around with him all the time, this one listing the ten best colleges in the country and showing the name of his son's college among the elect. I found myself wondering how many people throughout the country carried similar clippings—students desperately trying to assure themselves that they were just as good, just as knowledgeable, just as educated as their fellows attending colleges where they had failed of admittance; parents desperately trying to assure themselves that they were doing right by their children, that they were giving them the best, that they were not cheating them of their opportunity for the future.

CHAPTER 20

Standards–How You Could Get Them

If the colleges refuse to police themselves by standardizing the degrees they offer, and if the government is unable to, does that mean it cannot be done? Not at all. There is still the private sector. When the government is unable to act and the institution involved refuses to, the concerned private citizen must initiate the reform.

The question is, How do the various colleges compare in the effectiveness with which they perform their function? Does the student indeed derive more from his four years at Prestige than he would at State or Brannue? We speak glibly of the liberal arts college as offering an education, but isn't education actually a lifetime pursuit? It is a way of looking at the world around us, of judging experience and of understanding ourselves. It carries the implication of wisdom and sensitivity, penetration and discernment and discrimination. And the test of it is one's whole life.

What the college *does* offer is the knowledge and learning that help toward the attainment of the educated mind. And this knowledge and learning *can* be tested.

Fix a level of knowledge in a given field of study—English literature, physics, European history, mathematics—and a comprehensive examination can be devised that will indicate whether the student has attained it or not. Set the standard high so that it can be said with assurance that anyone who passes the examination has a good knowledge and understanding of the subject. If the examination were required of all college graduates, each in his own field of concentration, as law students take a bar exam and medical students a State Board, then we could judge the colleges by the percentage of their graduates who pass.

It would be a mistake to rank them on a mathematical basis, of course, since there are always accidental, adventitious considerations that affect any testing situation as well as subtle differences between one institution and another which will not be manifest in any formal examination but which are valid and important nevertheless. But such a set of examinations would show if the college is performing its basic function and if the prestige college is doing it markedly better than State or Brannue. If Prestige does show a marked superiority, then its reputation will be merited, and there would be some justification for its higher tuition fees—yes, and even for the tension and trauma involved in getting in. But I am inclined to believe that no such superiority would be demonstrated, and I base this assumption on the fact that graduates of all kinds of colleges are admitted to the graduate and professional schools of Prestige U. along with graduates of their own college, and the former have no difficulty in competing with the latter.

If, on the other hand, the prestige college did not show marked superiority over the rest, then it would be quickly seen that the prestige was purely a public relations kind of prestige having only snob value, and its influence on other colleges and on the educational system as a whole would in time be dissipated.

Obviously such a system of examinations could be established only by government ukase, and it's agreed that this is not likely. But what is to prevent a private foundation like the Ford or the Rockefeller or the Carnegie from offering such a series of examinations on a voluntary basis? It could probably be arranged in cooperation with the College Entrance Examination Board, who would run the examination, prepare the questions, and mark the papers. The examinee could even be charged a nominal fee to help defray the costs. It would be limited to those who hold a bachelor's degree and of necessity would be purely voluntary. The names of those who passed would be published, and the successful candidate would receive a certificate or diploma attesting that he had passed an examination in his major field of study, and perhaps one indicating a general knowledge of collegiate caliber outside his special field.

The examination would not be competitive since its purpose would be to demonstrate a knowledge of the subject rather than superiority over the rest of the candidates. There would be no trick questions or references to obscure points. In the English literature examination, for example, there would be no questions on the poetry of Simeon Suggs. The examination would be designed to test knowledge of basic principles and understanding of the subject as a whole. Conceivably, it might take several days. And of course, since it is in no sense a competition, it would not be graded, but like the bar examination or the Medical Board would be stamped either pass or fail.

It is not hard to see why the charitable foundation would be interested in such a venture; it is interested in education, and presumably in furthering any plan that could improve the American college. Although the complete restructuring of our educational system that is needed at this time is beyond the power of any private agency, or of any government other than a dictatorship for that matter, it is nevertheless possible for the private foundation to snub the system back into its proper direction by the application of the relatively small leverage that the voluntary examination could supply.

Let us suppose that a foundation could be found that would be willing to underwrite the initial costs of the experiment.

Now why would a college graduate want to take an examination of this kind? At first, no doubt, many would take it out of curiosity, or perhaps to test themselves. Mensa, for example, is an organization made up of people who consider themselves bright and want proof of it. It regularly schedules tests, for which the examinee pays, and which are the ticket of admission to the organization. Similarly, some might take the examination for diplomate in their special field, because it might help them in their future careers, either to get into a graduate school, or even to get a job. After all, since the graduate school is primarily interested in whether the applicant for admission has an adequate knowledge of the field in which he is going to do advanced work, the diplomate might find admission easy where formerly it had been impossible.

The graduates of the little-known school from an obscure section of the country would feel that the examination might be a means of overcoming the advantage of the prestige college and if he is permitted to take the examination as often as he likes, and if only the names of those who pass are publicized, as in the bar examination or medical specialty board exam, he would have no reason to fear it. The prestige of a degree from the Yale Law School or the Harvard Medical School does not depend on where one did one's undergraduate work. The status of one's graduate school replaces the status of one's college just as the status of the college overrides the status of one's prep school. Similarly, to be a diplomate in one's field might eventually have greater significance than the status of one's college. For this reason enthusiasm for the examination would probably come primarily from the smaller and less well-known colleges, and perhaps the graduates of the prestige colleges might hesitate. But after a while, failure to take the examination could indicate doubt of their own training and they would be shamed into it.

In any case, since it would give some reason for continuing one's studies after graduation, if only to prepare for the examination, it would have a good effect. Many students stop their reading and study as soon as they get their degrees. They have no incentive for continuing and after a while they get out of the habit. This system of voluntary examinations might provide just the incentive that some students need.

But suppose it catches on? Suppose it gains the same sort of acceptance that the College Board Examinations have now, or the examinations for Merit Scholarships? Then to be sure, a number of significant developments might take place. For one thing it would tend to equalize standards in American education. The graduate of the small college or the state college would not feel that he is handicapped. He would not have to apologize for the obscurity of his school. The fact that he was a diplomate in his field would give sufficient proof that his school was adequate even if relatively unknown.

One of the principal faults of the present system of free course election in our colleges today is that there may be little connection between the courses taken, even between those taken in the field of major concentration. In English, for example, the student may have taken a course in Anglo-Saxon, a writing course, a chunk of Victorian poetry, a segment of American literature, a course in Shakespeare's major tragedies. And except for a survey course he may have taken in the freshman or sophomore year, there is nothing to bind these courses together in a comprehensive view of the field. Since the examination for the diploma would of necessity be comprehensive and cover the entire field, there would be a tendency for the colleges to rearrange their courses to point for it. And this, in turn, would focus the attention of the faculty on their primary function of educating the student.

Events of recent months suggest that some method of certifying one's degree may be in order, to prove that it has any value at all. In my own college, as in so many colleges across the country, we embarked on a program of actively recruiting black students. We managed to get about fifty. But as is the case everywhere, few of them were able to meet our normal entrance requirements. So we did as other colleges have done and are doing; we gave them what was supposed to be an intensive course of instruction during the summer.

For me, this posed an immediate question: What kind of instruction could we give them in two months in the summer that would be equivalent to the four years of college preparatory work in high school? And if we could do all this in two months, was not the local school board wasting a lot of time by spreading two months' work over four years?

However, I was willing to assume that a special maturity they might have, in conjunction with a great need for higher education, might overcome their initial handicap, and that the two months of intensive study in academic modes of thought might furnish the kind of orientation that would counterbalance inadequate preparation. In any case, I thought it might be an interesting experiment and might develop in the black community a greater interest in learning than it had demonstrated heretofore.

A few days ago, however, the activist portion of our black students presented a manifesto to the faculty and administration, and then seized the administration building to call attention to their demands. These were: to establish a course in African studies, to increase the number of black members of the faculty, to engage a black dean, and to increase the number of black students to a fourth of the total enrollment, which in our case would mean approximately a thousand. To be sure, there was no violence, and the occupation was over that same night, but deans and other officers of the administration had been ordered out of their offices peremptorily, and some of them had been badly frightened. For men of their age this could have serious repercussions.

Of course, the administration agreed to do their best to increase the number of black students enrolled and to hire additional black faculty if possible. I am sure these promises were made in good faith, even though they were impossible of accomplishment to the degree that the black students demanded. It could only be done by reducing our standards of admission sharply, perhaps keeping only a minimum age limit.

Very well, what happens now? What happens when they take their final examinations and it is seen that they have not earned a passing grade? Do we then fail them? If they demand of the administration as a formal policy, or informally of the individual teacher, special concessions in the matter of grading, as in the matter of admission, will not concessions be made?

"You persuaded us to come, and we've spent the whole year here when we could have been working at some job and earning money, and now you tell us we flunked? It's a runaround, a trick of the white power structure, and we won't let you get away with it."

And the next year, and the next, and the next. And finally, commencement and the proud march in cap and gown in the academic procession, and striding to the platform for the final handshake with the president and the coveted degree.

How will the conscientious student, black or white, prove that the degree he received was truly earned? What will it be worth in applying for a job or for admission to a graduate school? How much status will it carry in the black community when it is no different in appearance from those of his classmates who were known to have done little or no work for it? For that matter, why would it not occur to the good student that he is a fool to prepare for his course exams or do the work required when he can pass and get his degree purely on the basis of his color?

Then, indeed, some method of certifying that one's degree is valid, that it is an earned degree, will not be merely useful but a necessity.

As I write, the school year has started again and already the whole unhappy business of demands and confrontations has begun. It may well be that the students, sensing a stiffening of the opposition, may exercise greater restraint. And it may merely spur them on to greater efforts. Whichever happens, the results will be unfortunate. If the administration and the professoriat win, the status quo will be maintained; and if the students win, the college will become a kind of adult education center, with which we have become familiar in recent years—a pleasant alternative once or twice a week to bowling, bridge, or TV watching. The teachers will all be interesting, which is to say entertaining; the courses will all be relevant, which is to say, they will deal with matters of the moment and will be dated by the time the student is ready to put them to use; and the credit system will be such that no student will fail, thus permitting large numbers of inadequately prepared students to achieve degrees at least as valid as those of the majority of our football players.

But if the administration and the professoriat should be able to resist, and maintain the status quo, it would be no victory either. I have spoken of an academic conspiracy, but of course the professor has been beguiled just as much as the student. True, his position seems much improved. His salary is higher and his teaching hours fewer, but he is forced to do research—not of some problem that interests him, but only research that is publishable, whether it interests him or not—and that on a competitive basis. And when he has reached the pinnacle of his ambition—the full professorship, tenure—and can stop, he still continues by force of habit.

But he had originally planned to teach, to change the minds of his students, to show them truth and beauty, to help them see life clearly and see it whole, and instead all he has to show for his life's work is a bibliography of papers in learned journals which have been read perhaps only by the board of editors and a few of his colleagues who deemed it politic. And now, even the pleasure that he might have had from this work is mixed with his bewilderment at the sudden change in the students who confront him—suspicious, questioning, angry.

What has happened is that all who are concerned—the administration, the faculty, the student and his parents, the general public—have drifted off their proper course and are suddenly in danger of foundering on the rocks. It is not a question of who will wear the gold braid and be in command, but rather a question of estimating the drift and getting back on course.

CHAPTER 21

By Way of Summation

In the last year, the situation on the American campus has grown markedly worse. The destruction of property, the arson, bombings, personal confrontations which result in injury to faculty and members of the administration, these came to a high point (thus far!) in a widely seen TV picture of students at Cornell marching out of an occupied building armed with rifles and shotguns. These can no longer be considered schoolboy games.

It is now obvious that the specific demands made by the pressure groups are not the real points at issue and that the initial confrontation is never as serious as the secondary one that follows administrative action of one sort or another. A pattern has evolved. First a small group, whose avowed intention is to harass, embarrass, hamper, and destroy if possible, makes a number of bold demands couched in the most peremptory terms

—obviously in order to evoke the least favorable and most antagonistic response. They then stage a demonstration that may take the form of a picket line or a sit-down to prevent access to one or more of the university buildings, or they may take possession of the building. They attract and even gain some measure of good-natured support from students, radical members of the faculty, onlookers, and friends from outside the college. The numbers initially attracted are rarely very large and their motives are mixed. For some it is a chance to witness or even to take part in some excitement as an escape from their drab environment —the group that under other circumstances would engage in panty raids. Some find themselves in sympathy with certain of the demands that are being made. For still others, the chance to confront authority in the comparative safety and anonymity of numbers has a strong appeal. There is one aspect of the situation however that is in a sense new to present-day campus rebellion: the participants are assured of either the approval or at least not the open disapproval of their parents. Their parents are all middle-class liberal-minded people who have urged their children to be concerned. Very well, this shows that they are concerned. They're not fighting to tear down goal posts after a football game; they're fighting for important things like peace and social justice and a new order.

Their parents have been assured by all the pundits and all the social commentators that this is what young people should be, and that American college youth has been way behind the college students of other countries in this respect. So even if they have some doubts, they do not voice them publicly, for they have also been repeatedly assured that this generation of college students, of young people in general, is superior in knowledge and hence of necessity in intelligence and wisdom to all other generations.

The first confrontation is little more than a nuisance. If it is the administration building that has been seized, there may be some fear for the safety of the college records; there may be some interference with the telephone switchboard; administration officials who have work to do may be kept from their desks.

If it continues for more than a day or two, its nuisance value increases by attracting the attention of more and more students who want to see what is going on and want to contribute their point of view, hopefully to a reporter and possibly even on TV. Classes and lectures are ignored and the work of the college grinds to a creaking halt.

In the crowds that are constantly milling about the campus, various points are developed, in agreement and in opposition, with the more articulate holding forth to whoever will listen to them. Ad hoc committees may be set up to press one point of view or another. There may be an occasional fracas when tempers get hot. Statements are issued, announcements are made, mimeographed flyers are distributed recounting the sequence of events: ". . . the response to the manifesto issued by the Committee of Concerned Students was completely disregarded by the Students for the Preservation of the College and in the now famous Reply of May 14 issued by the Student Faculty Coordinating Committee in which Point Seven was completely overlooked . . ."

As far as the students are concerned, the mood is still one of holiday, but the administration is growing restive. There have been editorials in the press and phone calls from members of the Board of Trustees reminding them of their duty. There have been letters and phone calls from alumni urging them to take steps. So finally they take steps. They suspend the ringleaders and threaten the rest with some form of disciplinary action.

Professors have theories as a dog has fleas and there are among the many "nonnegotiable" demands some points that coincide with their own thinking; so they take the opportunity to press these demands on their own. And of course, many of them have their own reasons for wanting to embarrass the administration. Then, too, the professor is just as susceptible as anyone else to the desire to be popular and to show that his mind is flexible. This means the president finds himself confronted not only by rebellious students, but by a rebellious segment of his faculty.

So he seeks to compromise by agreeing to those demands that

have faculty support and refusing those that have none. He can not very well say that the college is capitulating, that they are surrendering through fear without having fired a shot. So to save face, he explains that he is grateful that a group of concerned students has pointed out flaws in the system that the administration is now engaged in correcting, and that it proves what bright and serious and concerned students they have at the college now, and that he wouldn't have it any other way.

Now comes the second and more serious stage. The argument shifts from the original demands to a demand for amnesty for the student rebels. And here the students' position is bolstered by an irrefutable logic: if the students have rendered the college a service by pointing out its serious shortcomings, why should they be punished for it?

Now all those students and faculty who have a feeling for fair play become involved and the situation quickly worsens. Having wrung some concessions from the administration by a show of force, the rebels feel that they can win the rest, especially amnesty, by bolder and more violent action. At this point the local constabulary is brought in.

Between the student and the local police there has always been a certain antagonism. From the point of view of the police, college students are a bunch of rich kids, few of them local and many from out of state. They are noisy and rowdy and drive around the streets as if they owned the town. They are irreverent and disrespectful. Their very mode of dress, male and female, suggests that they consider themselves above the local mores. They are exempt from the draft, and instead of being grateful, they are scornful of the very government that granted them their privilege. When one of them does get arrested, his father may turn out to be a big shot who engages a high-priced lawyer, and the case ends up like as not with the arresting officer being blamed by the judge for having been overzealous.

From the point of view of the student, the police represent adult authority in its most visible and unpleasant form. They are big and tough and taciturn and don't even answer a simple question, like a request for a direction, graciously. Their language is uncultured and their knowledge limited. Their normal tones are sarcastic or truculent. Periodically, they are the subject of exposés, and the crooked cop is a common character in movies, TV, and detective fiction.

It is certain that any recalcitrance on the part of the students will be met by force, almost certainly more than necessary force, by the police. It is implicit in the antagonism between the two. Knowing this, why does the administration call in the police? First, because it is the most natural thing to do. Someone enters your premises illegally and it is the police that you look to for aid and redress. Second, because you are at an impasse with the students, a complete standoff, and the burden of getting the machinery of the college in motion rests with you. Third, because you feel like a fool being shut out of your own office. Fourth, because the pressures—from the alumni, from the board of trustees, from the older and more conservative members of the faculty, from the press—are all for recapturing the buildings and reestablishing law and order. And fifth, perhaps, because you hope that your adjurations to the civil authority to exercise restraint will be heeded and that the maneuver will go off without a hitch and without physical resistance by the embattled students.

But of course it doesn't.

There are always some students who, presuming on the safety in their numbers, refuse to go willingly. After their earlier heroics it is embarrassing to walk out meekly on their own power. "If they want to get me out, they'll have to carry me." So they slump to the floor, and the police drag them out bodily, sometimes by the feet so their heads bump along the floor, at least as long as they are not in sight of photographers or TV cameras. Perhaps too, the students confuse them with the campus police who are in the Dogberry and Verges or Keystone Cop tradition. Curiously enough, the leaders are usually not hurt—the TV cameras are apt to be trained on them.

The shock of the completely predictable confrontation with the police brings about an overwhelming sympathy for the students and equally overwhelming condemnation for the administration from the great mass of students and faculty who had hitherto remained on the sidelines. Once again committees are set up, student committees, faculty committees, joint committees of students and faculty, and once again resolutions are passed. Student mass meetings are held at which the more liberal or progressive faculty members are present and are called upon to speak.

Then comes the formal meeting of the faculty with a committee of student observers in attendance and crowds of students waiting outside in the hall and on the steps. The vote will be in favor of the students' position—the waiting students would not permit anything else—but in the resolution that is hastily framed there will be a clause piously repudiating the use of violence to call the attention of the college to the evils which could not have been called to their attention except by the use of violence. If the president does not resign, he will make a speech accepting the mandate of the vote of the faculty, congratulate the students for these very tangible proofs of their concern for important issues, admit that the college was slow in implementing changes that had been under study for several months, and then end by explaining that the college is now stronger and better as a result of the "dialogue" which had been carried on and for which reason he was granting complete amnesty to all. There is loud applause and cheers and the college settles down to peace and quiet—until the next time.

One segment of the college community is never heard from, and that is the parent of the student. He is not consulted by anyone—not by the student or the faculty or the administration. He takes no part in the meetings and passes no resolutions. He and his wife are perhaps too busy working to support their son at college. His attitude is curiously ambivalent. In public, he no doubt supports his son and condones his activism. "You got to hand it to those kids. They're involved. They're concerned. They're not like we were in college, just bent on having a good time and to hell with the rest of the world. And look what a mess we made of it for them. I mean, this war and all this pollution, and our cities decaying and all the rest of it. But these kids—they care. Maybe their methods are . . . but you know damn well you can't get anything done unless you go out and fight for it. Look at the colored. Of course, I'm a little old-fashioned and . . . but they're smart, so I guess they know what they're doing."

But privately, at home, with just his wife there, he is far less certain. He has made serious sacrifices to send his son to college because he knows that it is necessary for his future. By instinct and training he cannot approve of his son's straggly beard and long, unkempt hair, the chain and pendant around his neck, his generally slovenly appearance. The long hair and the chain he secretly considers effeminate; the beard, not a sign of masculinity, but rather a disregard for his personal appearance.

He cannot possibly view with equanimity the chance of his son's being suspended or expelled. He cannot be pleased to hear that his son was arrested and spent a night in jail. He cannot approve of the risk his son is taking of having his head split open. He does not approve of the war, much less of his son taking part in it, but he has little hope that the rebellion on the campus will change things much, and it occurs to him that if his son is expelled, he will lose his draft deferment and be called up immediately.

And yet his son can silence his criticism instanter by suggesting that he can leave college if his father doesn't like the way he is behaving there. This seems to the father the worst tragedy of all. He has so much of his life and effort invested in his son's college career. It is not merely the explanations he will have to make to his friends, there is also the knowledge that for his son to leave school would be to jeopardize his entire future. So he remains silent, consoling himself with the thought that his son is young, just a boy, and when he gets a little older, he'll come around and see things realistically.

That perhaps is the key to the situation—the student is just a boy. Regardless of his size and age, the student is still a boy. And therein lies the strength of his position. It is his boyness that enables him to challenge the college authorities, the Establishment. It is the strength of weakness like that which permits Peru or North Korea to seize an American vessel with impunity. The strong, when provoked by the very weak, hesitate to retaliate—like the grown man who is spattered with mud by a child.

The small group of radicals who seize a college building and hold it for days and weeks against the wishes of the administration and the vast majority of the student body—is it because they are supermen? Because they are stronger than the greatly superior numbers whom they have excluded? No, it is because they are obviously and demonstrably weaker.

Then too, in our youth-oriented society where middle age is pitied if not ridiculed; where important executives of major industry are retired at sixty-five not because they cannot continue their work, but to make way for younger men coming up; where age is synonymous with hardening of the arteries and softening of the brain; where mature people try to prove their eternal youth by copying the tastes of the young in music, dancing, and dress while the young people like very young children dress up in their grandfather's clothes and their grandfather's beards and spectacles; in a society so oriented there is bound to be the feeling that the young are right. They can always outshout you and you can no longer discipline them.

The most tragic aspect of the contemporary campus scene, however, is the situation of the black student. Himself but recently admitted by a special reduction of the normal admissions requirements and in most cases after an intensive recruiting drive in the black community, he now demands that more be admitted in large, and under the circumstances, impossible numbers; that black faculty be recruited in proportion; that courses in black literature and black history whose subject matter they will pass on be given by teachers whom they will select. They are supported in their demands by large numbers of the student body and the faculty because of guilt feelings or even because of an honest conviction that something must be done to bring the black community to equality with the rest of our society and that anything is better than nothing.

It might be an interesting experiment to determine if our present system of college preparatory subjects is indeed necessary to carry on collegiate work. It is possible that living in a ghetto where the pressures and tensions are extreme may have the effect of endowing the black student with a special maturity that permits him to grasp intuitively what his white classmate learned in school; that his struggle in a difficult environment has sharpened his mind so that he understands instinctively the subtleties of literature, the sweep of history, the complexities of scientific theory. But an idea that runs so directly counter to educational experience over the centuries could be only an experiment to be carefully watched and the results scrupulously analyzed. And if an experiment, then common sense requires that it be small and that the college should not waste its major resources on what is so contrary to prevailing thought.

Much more likely it will be found that the obvious is probably true and that advanced learning requires preliminary learning. A certain amount of factual knowledge and basic techniques is just plain necessary. Much of the learning in the secondary school may not be of importance in and of itself in collegiate study, but the mental habits that were developed during the learning process are.

What bothers me most about the readiness of the college community to back the black students in their demands is that essentially it is patronizing. Back of the insistence that black demands for special study programs taught by special teachers to students admitted under special rules is the sense that ordinary studies under ordinary teachers are above their capacity.

This is not true. The black race is not inferior, but, under prevailing conditions, the majority have not had the chance to learn normally. A black student, however, who has taken a trade course in high school, been truant for long periods, and then been graduated as much to get rid of him as because he has completed the work, can probably not carry on liberal arts work in college. I do not believe that a white student could either. And conversely, I am certain, on the basis of my own observation, that a black student who *has* undergone the normal preparation for college will do as well as a student of any other racial strain.

During the Depression I worked for several years as a substitute teacher in the Boston school system. I reported every day at the offices of the School Committee and waited patiently to be sent anywhere in the system to take the place of a teacher who had called in sick. I might spend a day or a week, or even several months at a school, and I was sent at one time or another to most of the schools in the system. I soon learned that the teacher depended on the sanction of the parent in order to function. In those areas where the parents were firmly behind the teacher, the discipline was good and as a direct result the teaching was good. In those areas where the discipline was bad, teaching was well-nigh impossible, and it could be directly attributed to the lack of concern for education by the parents.

I know nothing of the Negro schools in the South, but I am willing to accept as true that all the while they were operating under the "separate and equal" clause, they were separate but not equal; that in fact they were totally inadequate. But if the situation in Boston was typical of Northern cities generally, then the education offered was the same for all segments of the city. The buildings were of the same type, the teachers were appointed from the same list, and the curriculum and teaching materials were the same.

The difference was that in one school the teacher could teach because the parents of the children were insistent that they learn, and in the other he could not because they weren't. If the buildings of the latter were shabbier, if the walls were marked and the desks broken, it was because all children are destructive, but in the poor schools they could be destructive with relative impunity so there was more of it. If the absentee rate of teachers was higher in the schools in the Negro areas than the average for the city, it was because the work was harder and placed a greater strain on the nervous energy of the teacher.

It is pointless to argue that there are teachers who are truly dedicated and are therefore able to establish rapport with students who are unruly and manage to interest them in learning their lessons. These are teaching geniuses and by definition the genius is rare; there can never be enough of them to staff a school.

Nor does it help to develop a special curriculum, designed to insure the interest of the children to the point where they will accept the work involved with eagerness. The learning process involves protracted attention and tedium and hard work. It may very well be that the mental discipline thereby developed is the most valuable part of the training. The simple fact of the matter is that there is no royal road to education.

Nor is it helpful to excuse the black parent for his lack of interest and concern because of the special hardships society has imposed on him. It is a sociological fact, but it cannot be offered as an alternative to college preparatory training. It could, however, justify special arrangements on college fees. Of all conditions restricting admission to college, lack of funds, especially in the case of Negro candidates, should not be controlling. This concession should be made. But as a matter of fact, it has already been made by colleges throughout the country. The demand that large numbers of blacks be recruited and admitted without examination of any kind, however, should not be acceded to, if for no other reason than that it is totally fraudulent; the faculty members who insist on it, know this. It is no favor to the black community or to the black student to give him a stone when he asks for bread, to give him credits for courses he has not passed, to give him a degree he has not earned. Whatever practical or monetary value attaches to the degree at present will be quickly dissipated and will be as useful to him as a diploma bought in a secondhand store.

In the other demands—for courses in black literature and black history taught by black teachers, in an African Studies program supervised by a black director of their choosing—there is a feeling that it is a cop-out. If the black students were adequately prepared and felt that they could compete with white classmates on equal terms, I do not think that they would be either so insistent or even overinterested in these courses. Certainly, any student who was interested could study them on his own.

In a successful social revolution power must change hands as the situation changes. The kind of people who incite a society to radical change, the forceful charismatic leaders who can inspire their people to hazard what security they have for the initial gamble, rarely have the personality or the habits of mind for the systematic and methodical day-to-day business that becomes all important once the revolution has established itself. If power does not pass from the one to the other, what has been won can very easily be lost. As dramatic confrontations give way to the slow and tedious task of consolidating ground gained, the ardor of the revolutionary tends to cool and he either loses interest and drifts away, or remembering the intoxication of heroic battles, he seeks out new and more radical leaders to follow.

Although it is only natural that the angry young man of the Negro community should prefer continued violent confrontation, the time has actually come, at least on the academic front, for the slow hard work of consolidation. Continued violent confrontation on the campus now leads not to new gains but to a stiffened opposition where the gains of the past may well be lost. The one great concession that the black student should not be barred from a college education for lack of funds has been won. Indeed, many colleges had already made the concession before the black students demanded it. In most cases it was the basis for their own presence on the campus. But it is now time to put this privilege to a proper use by arranging for adequately prepared young people to take advantage of it. And that means improving teaching conditions in the schools of the ghetto.

Sociological conditions in the ghetto remain very much as they were. But there could be a true sociological revolution and the Negro would be able to take his proper and equal place in our society if a band of involved young men and women made a concerted effort to improve their schools by backing up the teachers, black or white; if they urged the parents of the children to do the same, by encouraging youngsters to study now that there is reasonable chance of a college education and the advancement that it could lead to; if they appealed to the youngsters' pride to make it on their merits rather than on their color which is merely the other side of racial discrimination.

Under the stress of the campus rebellions, many changes have been made in recent months in the structure of the college. In most cases, these have been made in the heat of battle, as it were, as concessions to the demands of a radical and violent minority. But regulations formulated in haste are frequently repented at leisure. I see nothing in the changes that have been made so far that is likely to improve the institution. For the most part they seem to be on the order of concessions to the students for a greater share in the governing of the college. I cannot see that this gives the needed change in direction; it only puts a less experienced driver at the wheel. It makes the college more responsive to the fads and passions of the moment when it should act as a brake on them. In our fast-moving and ever-changing society, the college was an instrument of slow time, standing as a bastion of the eternal verities against the whims and fancies of the moment. I cannot see that our society will profit by eliminating it.

Index

C

D

E

3 1625 00022 4185

DATE DUE
DISCA
GAYLORD
PRINTED IN U.S.A.